FAMILY ALBUM

Edwardian Life in the Lake Counties

FAMILY ALBUM

Edwardian Life in the Lake Counties

JOHN SATCHELL

SUTTON PUBLISHING LIMITED

First published in the United Kingdom in 1996 by
Sutton Publishing Ltd • Phoenix Mill • Far Thrupp • Stroud • Gloucestershire

British Library Cataloguing in Publication Data
A catalogue record for this book is available from the British Library.

ISBN 0-7509-1049-6

Typeset in Perpetua
Typesetting and origination by
Sutton Publishing Limited.
Printed in Great Britain by
Butler & Tanner, Frome, Somerset.

CONTENTS

PREFACE

The collection of photographs here presented contributes a small but significant addition to the archives of Kendal and its Cumbrian hinterland from the opening years of the twentieth century between the end of the Boer War and the beginning of the Great War. Stephen Shaw, a locally distinguished architect responsible for most of Kendal's best Victorian buildings, lived then in Stricklandgate with his sick wife, his son Malcolm, also an architect, and his daughter Margaret. Between running the household and her busy social life, Margaret spent much of her spare time photographing the family, their friends, their tea parties, picnics and outings. When by the merest chance the collection came into the author's hands, having been lost for many years, it lacked all but a minimum of labelling and seemed at first to be mostly unidentifiable. One photograph, published by the *Westmorland Gazette*, was however recognised by Stephen Shaw's grandson, Mr Ian Shaw, and from then on many happy hours of detective work were spent by the Shaw family, revealing the identity of many of the subjects, both people and places. Without their kind help the collection would have been impossible to understand and I acknowledge their enthusiastic collaboration with gratitude.

As always, the Local History librarians of the public library in Kendal and the archivists of the Kendal branch of the Cumbria Record Office gave their unstinting help on local places and history, and Abbot Hall Art Gallery provided valuable advice on furnishings, paintings and interior design. The Gallery of English Costume of Manchester City Art Galleries kindly advised on costume and many other libraries, museums and individuals, acknowledged on pp. 151 and 152, kindly assisted in various specialist fields. I thank them all for their help.

1

THE COLLECTION

In the summer of 1990, a large wooden box of glass plate photographic negatives of unknown origin turned up in a house in Kendal. The bottom of the box had all but rotted away, and the first step towards examining them was to invert the whole lot into another box and sort them in reverse order. The upper layer was a solid mass of wet glass plates welded together with a sticky gelatinous mass of photographic emulsion. It went straight into the dustbin. Below this was a stratum of plates which, when prized apart, revealed blotched and mottled groups of ladies wearing Edwardian hats, dimly discernible through dendritic webs of fungal mould. These too were quickly binned. The next horizon comprised a layer of decomposed envelopes, bottomless cardboard boxes and damp and spotted plates, some cracked, some irremovably glued to interleaving paper. Carefully separated and cleaned, many of these showed more groups of ladies with strangely elongated chins and lofty intellectual brows where the emulsion had contracted across the plate. The best of this layer was set aside for further consideration. Below it were fifty boxes and seventy envelopes of plates, damp, thick with dirt and dust but retrievable. After many hours of cleaning and drying about 750 plates were recovered out of the whole collection, probably of over a thousand.

Most of the boxes and envelopes carried a note of the subject, place and date of the plates within, the dates mainly between 1900 and 1908 with some up to 1916. Where the plates were in individual envelopes and the places recorded could be identified, the description and the place generally corresponded and some reliance could therefore be placed on the dates and identity of the people recorded. However, many of the boxes had been reused or added to after the original caption had been written. Much cross-checking was needed to confirm the information given but, despite this, some misidentifications may have gone undetected.

When the locations written on the boxes and envelopes had been listed it became clear that the material could be roughly classified into a Kendal group, a group centred on the parishes of Rosley and Westward near Wigton, Lake District beauty spots, various places around the periphery of the Lake District, and a miscellaneous group of holiday photographs. Two groups, centred on a Sawrey family and a Rosley family, were explored and produced interesting information, but failed to provide a coherent link between the various groups. There were, however, five lots of plates which had captions referring to either the photographer or the caption writer as 'I' or

Jack Jordan's wedding, 1905. The distortion is caused by moisture softening the photographic emulsion.

'me'. One read 'Mother and I, 1901' and another 'Mother, Aunt Elijah and Me'. 'Mother' was a very individual woman with sharp features and hair tied back off a prominent forehead who was readily recognisable in several other photographs. In many of them she was outside a house on which the number 157 was clearly readable, and the best of these was sent to the *Westmorland Gazette* who kindly published it with a request for information. The response was immediate, the first caller announcing that the house was 157 Stricklandgate, Kendal, and that the people outside it were his grandparents, Mr and Mrs Stephen Shaw; his father, Malcolm Shaw; his aunt Margaret Shaw, later Mrs John Bewley; and their dog Prince (for the Shaw family tree see p. 150). The caller was Mr Ian Shaw, a prominent Kendal businessman who, over twenty-five years before, had found the collection of photographic plates while clearing his recently deceased grandfather's house. Recognising their interest as an archive of Kendal history, he gave them to Jack O'Connor, author of *Memories of Old Kendal*, and frequent contributor to the *Westmorland Gazette* with nostalgic articles on the Kendal of his youth. Mr O'Connor died shortly afterwards and his house was sold and cleared, except for a small residue of his effects which was taken down to the cellar. There the photographs remained until 1990 when they were discovered, quite by chance, by the author. Despite the lapse of nearly ninety years since most of them were taken, Mr Shaw was able to supply enough information about the central characters to link the various groups into a coherent collection.

Stephen Shaw and his wife Jane, his son Malcolm, his daughter Sarah Margaret (Maggie) and Prince outside 157 Stricklandgate, Kendal.

No. 157 Stricklandgate, home of the Shaw family, seen from the door of St Thomas's church as members of the congregation arrive for a service.

2

THE SHAWS OF KENDAL

The four members of the Shaw family appear equally in the photographs, and the collection itself provides no evidence as to which of them was the main photographer. One picture shows Margaret holding a camera and, although that must have been taken by someone else, there is clear evidence from Margaret's diaries, two of which have survived in the possession of the family, that she was indeed the principal photographer. The two diaries, for 1909 and 1912, open with the address of the Halifax Photographic Company and record taking 'snapshots' at Rosley House and half a dozen other locations; developing plates with her friend Mary Littlewood; attending a lecture on colour photography at Kendal Museum; and visiting a photographic exhibition in Lancaster. A few of the envelopes and boxes containing the glass plates are labelled 'Malcolm's Photographs' and a few are written in his hand, but the great majority are in the same hand as the diaries, undoubtedly 'Maggie's'.

The diaries are mainly a record of events, friends and relatives and contain little comment or opinion, but they nevertheless provide many clues to the circumstances of Margaret's life. Her mother, Jane Shaw, died in November 1909 and Margaret became effectively the housewife of 157 Stricklandgate. Like other housewives, she was much occupied in the kitchen and her diaries record making gingerbread, raspberry jam, crab apple jelly and lemon cheese, a hunt to buy strawberries in Staveley and Garnett Bridge, and the drama of Christmas Day 1909, when 'oven got on fire when goose was in'.

The household supported a succession of servants: 'Dorothy', Mrs Davis and Annie Garth in 1909 and Mrs Hully in 1912. Papering the little bedroom and laying the oilcloth was a job for Malcolm and Margaret, as was painting the dining room, an event in which the cat Fluff was lost before turning up the next day in the rolled-up carpet. Besides domestic chores, Margaret kept the office open when Stephen and Malcolm Shaw, both architects, were out, and occasionally she acted as Quantity Surveyors' clerk for the practice. Mornings were often taken up marketing but the main afternoon occupation was taking tea, generally about three times a week with guests and three afternoons visiting. Bicycle rides to friends in Longsleddale, Brigsteer, Underbarrow, and the neighbouring

Sarah Margaret (Maggie) Shaw (left) with her friends the Misses Stevenson, 1905. Maggie wears an 'aesthetic' dress – loose, flowing and graceful.

villages generally concluded with teas, as did afternoon meetings of the Sewing Circle, the Primrose League, the Band of Hope and an 'Insect Tea' at Laurel Bank, perhaps a prototype beetle drive.

A varied programme of supper parties, concerts and other entertainments filled most winter evenings, a night spent roller skating with Malcolm and Gertie Sharpe following hard on an evening chapel lecture entitled 'Should Men Fear Death?'. There were lots of lectures, at the Museum and at the Wesleyan Chapel, variously informative, improving or uplifting. Margaret's diaries record 'Prince Charlie made Supper', Nicholas Nickleby, Peru, the Congo, Kingsley, Bunyan and Mr Warberry's elocutionary recital! On evenings spent in, Margaret and Malcolm occasionally played Kuhn-Kan, a nursery card game of Mexican origin rather like 'Rummy' and popular in Edwardian families.

Like most middle-class Edwardian ladies Margaret had been taught music, and she played the organ occasionally for weddings and chapel events. Her diaries mention an evening at 157 Stricklandgate when they 'Had music etc'; another when she 'Played at Gillingate, Mrs Tarpin sang'; and visits to the Mary Wakefield Festival concerts, the Children's Festival

Concert, the Grammar School concert and the Railway Men's concert.

Church occupied much of Sunday, often a service in the morning and evening and a bible class in the afternoon. Margaret's regular church was the Wesleyan church on the corner of Burneside Road, but occasionally she attended the Friends' meeting, All Hallows church, the Brethren church, St John's, and, for harvest festivals and carols, St Thomas's. She records collecting funds for church missions and attending the functions of the Wesleyan Guild, congregational meetings, lectures, socials, sales of work, outings, 'Hot Pot' and 'Potato Pie' suppers. At the farewell party for the Wesleyan minister, Mr Gray, and his wife, Margaret presented them with books and made her first speech. In the interregnum before the next minister was appointed, the church had visiting preachers including Mr Campbell of Haltwhistle, recorded in the diary as 'no good', but when the Rev. Scott Hendry was appointed Margaret spent two days collecting subscriptions for a 'Gown and Lunch', and two days preparing for and attending his induction and the reception which followed it.

Garden sale, Rosemont, Kendal, 1907. Margaret Shaw is at the far right with her camera. It was of a type which could be loaded with up to a dozen glass plates before an expedition as an alternative to the recently invented roll-film camera.

Windermere, 1900. Margaret Shaw's plate camera is on the seat.

Maggie on holiday crossing the River Trent with her bicycle, under the eye of Mr John Haslam, farmer and ferryman at Carlton on Trent, 1904.

Between these stirring events there were whist drives and bridge parties, weddings and funerals, friends to see off at Liverpool, the Agricultural Show, boating on Windermere, family to be visited at Rosley, Ackworth Old Scholars' Meeting, the opening of the bandstand in Abbot Hall Park and a trip to see Mr Wakefield's aeroplane. Even theatre found a place in Kendal life, and with Malcolm she saw *Raffles, The Chocolate Soldier, The Merry Widow* and a performance called *Drama of Dobsons*. Fortunately for her photographic hobby in this action-packed life, Margaret enjoyed good health and recorded nothing worse than occasional colds and headaches, a nose that needed a few stitches after a fall downstairs and a plumstone that went the wrong way.

Founded by Robert Shaw of Serpentine Road, Kendal, an eighteenth-century designer/builder, the architectural practice of the Shaw family designed many of Kendal's most important Victorian buildings. Two of his three sons, Richard Carradus, Stephen and Christopher, and his grandson Malcolm, all became architects. Richard Carradus Shaw built Gawith Buildings in Highgate, the building on the corner of Branthwaite Brow and Stramongate, Castle Street cemetery and chapel, and Laburnum Bank and a number of other houses in Castle Road, before an untimely death in 1862 at the age of thirty-one. Stephen Shaw, FRIBA, was much more prolific and built most of the best buildings erected in Kendal between 1870 and the end of the century. One of his earliest designs was for

Stephen Shaw (left) on holiday on Loch Long, 1900.

his own house, 157 Stricklandgate, of which the neo-Georgian front survives with its original fanlight and a few distinctively panelled doors inside. Perhaps the best known of his buildings are the Grammar School, the conversion of the old White Hall to the present Town Hall and the Zion chapel. Besides these he built Bannel Head; Stonecross, until recently used as a youth hostel; the Tower Buildings in Stramongate with a touch of the French chateau style; the Market Place public library, of which the front has been transferred to Sandes Avenue; the Sawyers' Arms, combining an elegant façade with a cosy pub-scale interior; Tudor House, in a rustic mock-Tudor style; Waterloo House in Finkle Street, with elements of 'Arts and Crafts' design; and in the same year, 1908, the charming motor house at 23 Castle Road. Some of his best buildings – Jordan's Granary, the Presbyterian Chapel on Sandes Avenue, the County Mews and two shops on the south corner of Finkle Street and Highgate, have only recently been demolished.

An idea of the sumptuousness of Stephen Shaw's designs, when given his head, can be gained from an account in the 1908 *Westmorland Gazette* of Waterloo House, Finkle Street, Kendal, built for £2,850 exclusive of the site. 'The walls are founded upon massive blocks of limestone; and the freestone dressings, from the Prudham Quarries, are polished, cut and moulded in the most pleasing manner, and filled in with a beautiful quality of Kendal Fell white limestone. The panels under the windows, together with the panel of pilasters, the full length of the building, are intended to be filled in with polished Shap granite and Minton's celebrated tiles. The lower pilaster capitals will be handsomely carved in imitation of flowers, fruit, etc. and the space between the moulded strings of chamber windows forms a polished freestone sign, and bears the words "Waterloo House" in bold relief. It is intended to cover the face of the letters with gold leaf. At the front of the shop, there will be a great display of plate glass; the eight handsome panes of the shop windows containing upwards of 400 superficial feet. The shop front will be cast iron of beautiful design and workmanship by Messrs Bellhouse of Manchester, the well-known makers and will be decorated and gilded with gold leaf.'

The description continues with the interior: its immense size; the beautiful double staircase with its polished Spanish mahogany balustrading; the panelled and decorated plaster work; the cast-iron pillars with their capitals all 'picked out in colour and gilded'; the coach work finish of the counters and show cases; and the 50 foot hoist running from cellar to attics.

The mutilated façade of the upper floors of this spectacular Edwardian building survives: the ground floor, ignominiously gutted, has been replaced by the crude functionalism of a cut-price grocers' chain-store. The collection includes two photographs which show the interior of Stephen Shaw's office at 45 Highgate with notices of building land for sale, drawing instruments and piles of drawings. The premises are still used by an architectural practice. Stephen Shaw died in 1930 and is buried in Castle Street cemetery.

Yard 43, Highgate, Kendal, 1900. The office of the Shaw architectural practice, no. 45, was above the grocers, C.R. Pennington, and was approached from Yard 43. The Highgate Pharmacy survives, but no longer advertises sheep dip.

Underwood, Queen's Road, Kendal. A Stephen Shaw house and home of John Brunskill, general draper, dress and mantle maker, of 1, 3, and 5 Mercers' Lane. Stephen Shaw also built Hollin Garth, Prospect and Brantfell on Queen's Road and a number of the larger houses on Greenside, Castle Road and Sunnyside. Margaret and Malcolm Shaw played bridge here.

The office interior of the Shaw architectural practice.

Another view of the office.

Malcolm Graham Shaw at 157 Stricklandgate, 1907. Having been brought up in an architectural family, Malcolm was sent for his own training to the firm of a cousin, George Brown and Son, builders, general contractors and monumental sculptors, of Newark. According to family tradition, he had some part, while he was there, in building the Quorn Hunt Kennels. His subsequent work in Kendal was purely commercial and shows little of his father's interest in design. The extension to Kendal museum housing the taxidermy collection, the laundry on Shap Road, garages in Kirkland, the doctors' surgery in Stricklandgate and the village halls at Crosthwaite, Holme and Staveley provide examples of his work. He designed and modernised council housing for a number of local authorities and was retained by a number of breweries, on whose behalf he modernised some twenty public houses in Kendal and many more in the vicinity. The building he considered his major work, best proportioned and most pleasingly designed, was the Technical School, now the Allen Technical College in Sandes Avenue, the foundation stone of which was laid in 1912 when he was thirty-two. In 1926, at the age of forty-five, Malcolm married Phyllis Watson of Eden Mount, Horncop Lane, Kendal.

Jane Shaw, Stephen Shaw's wife, appears in the photographs up to the time of her death in 1909, and is seen here at 157 Stricklandgate. As Jane Graham she was born at Sebergham, near Rosley, both small Cumberland parishes near Wigton. Her sister, Miss Esther Graham, known to Margaret Shaw as 'Aunt Ettie', farmed Broadmoor, a traditional Rosley stock-raising farm where the Shaws spent frequent summer holidays. Margaret's diaries recall them leaving Kendal on the 9.36 train to Penrith, travelling on via Carlisle to Curthwaite on the Maryport line, and being collected by Dick Osborne in the trap in time for tea at Broadmoor.

Mrs Jane Shaw in a motorised basket chair. Malcolm Shaw's consuming passion was motorbikes. BC 197, a Leicester number, was perhaps registered by him when he was working in Newark.

3

THE ROSLEY CONNECTION

Margaret Shaw eventually married into the Bewley family from the neighbouring farm of Causa Grange, and her photographs show interesting contrasts between the life style of these yeoman farmers and that of her friends, the Rookes of Rosley House, an elegant Georgian house built on the profits of the cotton trade.

Margaret's diaries describe a number of visits to Rosley where, in the autumn of 1912, she spent a month at Broadmoor, her aunt's house, with her friend May Sharpe. Their days were filled with long walks to Barrow Mill, Caldbeck, Dalston, Warnell Fell, Sebergham and Welton, the last a round trip of 12 miles. Cycle rides, shopping expeditions to Wigton and Carlisle, tea with most of the neighbours within a walking distance of about 5 miles, numerous tea and supper parties at Rosley House, and local events including a meet at Rosley and a horse sale at Wigton filled other days. Some were too wet to go out and were spent writing letters. As a diary entry put it, 'Nothing startling happened today.'

On one spring visit Margaret combined a few days at Broadmoor with a week at Kirkbride, about 5 miles from Rosley and, in July, Malcolm and Margaret spent a long weekend at Broadmoor helping in the hayfield. Stephen and Jane Shaw appear in the photographs of many of these visits, outside the inn at High Hesket, at Barrow Mill and picnicking at Silloth.

The arrival of the railways in the North American prairies opened Britain's ports to shiploads of wheat at prices well below the cost of home production. Meat production too became uneconomic as Argentina, Australia and New Zealand flooded the market with cheap beef and mutton brought over in refrigerated ships. By 1894 wheat prices were lower than at any time in the previous 150 years and farmers could neither pay their labourers a living wage nor repair their cottages. At an average 10*s* a week a farm labourer's wage was about half what could be earned in the town and cities and, in a massive rural exodus, labourers left the countryside in their thousands. Land prices fell, village life declined and by 1901 there was an acute shortage of labour on the land.

Rosley, on a droving road from Scotland and the centre of a great cattle fair, was essentially graziers' country. Some oats were grown, mainly for the horses, and a few potatoes and turnips but, with the prevailing high rainfall, good grass and lots of it was the main crop. As the farming economy collapsed, so too did Rosley Fair. At one time attracting 2,000 cattle and 500 horses a day, it struggled on with a few horse sales until the Great War.

Hesket Newmarket. This small market town about 5 miles south-west of Rosley once had a weekly market and many summer and autumn cattle fairs. As agriculture declined, business moved out to the larger commercial and banking centres and it is now a village within the parish of Caldbeck. The square, white building in the photograph was built in the late eighteenth century as a moot hall, approached by the outside staircase, with a coach house below. It subsequently served as a butcher's shop, a petrol station and a garage. The eighteenth-century market cross to the left has an iron ring for tethering bulls set into the road beside it. In modern times the pillars have been rebuilt and the moot hall pebble-dashed.

New Yeat Inn, Castle Sowerby, built in 1836 in the heyday of Hesket Newmarket's cattle fairs at a road junction on the way to Penrith. It had a smithy (left), eleven fields and a cottage (right), now drastically rebuilt. The inn ceased trading in the early 1960s and is now a private house. Stephen Shaw (standing), Mrs Shaw and Malcolm are waiting for the farrier to replace a cast hind shoe.

'Young and the bull': a Shorthorn at Petteril Bank, 1905. The long-broken downspout, the improvised lean-to shed and the unkempt farmyard are typical of the small tenanted farmsteads of the period.

Billy Rooke of Rosley House, 1902.

Mary Rooke with Billy and her mother outside Rosley House, 1906. Rosley House, a modest country house built in a late Georgian style, is first mentioned in surviving records in 1838. It had been occupied before the time of the photographs by several generations of the Rooke family, small yeoman farmers who had acquired wealth by marriage with the Pattinsons of Wigton, cotton manufacturers at Brookside Works in Water Street. Used to supporting their gentry life style on tenants' rents, the Rookes were hard hit by the depression and William Wharton Rooke kept going by mortgaging his property up to the hilt. In 1894 he mortgaged Rosley House, an estate called Intack and twenty-two fields for £1,350 and in 1895 he borrowed another £1,000. In 1896, having repaid his debts, he remortgaged Rosley House and Intack together with Stocks Farm, the Wheatsheaf Inn and farm, the Crown and Anchor Inn and three fields, for £4,750. Rosley House was still mortgaged when his wife, Mary Eleanor Rooke, inherited it at his premature death in 1902. In the same year Mrs Rooke had a son, Joseph William, generally known as 'Billy'. Malcolm Shaw befriended Billy, who eventually moved to Kendal where he became an insurance agent. He died in 1966.

Billy in his tam-o-shanter.

Billy in his father's riding boots, 1909.

Dick Osborne at the pump, Broadmoor Farm. Contrasting with the life style of Rosley House was that of the tenant farmers with rents to pay, likened to eels which 'grow accustomed to being skinned'. Miss Esther Graham, Jane Shaw's sister and tenant of Broadmoor was one of these. In 1898 she had an almost complete dispersal sale of her farm stock, the sale bill of which survives in the possession of her family. It describes her as 'widely known as a very prominent breeder of Shorthorns, having during the last twenty years obtained scores of prizes at the local shows'. Her stock included '42 Head of Pure Bred Shorthorn Cattle', possessing 'immense Breeding and Dairy qualities'; 10 Clydesdale Horses; 119 sheep, mainly Grey-faced and Cheviot hogs and some Border Leicester ewes and tups; and three pigs. There were stacks of hay and oats, carts, ploughs, turnip cutters and all the implements and impedimenta of a mixed stock farm.

On her retirement in 1914 she had a final clearance sale, this time with a smaller stock of twenty cattle, four horses, a few ducks and hens, some oats, hay and potatoes, her farming and dairy equipment and her surplus household goods. Her cows sold for about £20 each, heifers for about £12 and bullocks for £9, about a thirtieth to a fortieth of today's prices. The gross yield of the sale was approximately £600, equivalent perhaps to about £20,000 today.

Miss Esther Graham, Margaret Shaw's 'Aunt Ettie', at 157 Stricklandgate, 1905.

Baking day at Broadmoor.

William Holliday, miller and farmer of Barrow Mill, Southwaite, with Mrs Holliday and Stephen Shaw. The house is now 2 Barrow Mill Cottages. Barrow Mill, a small corn mill on the River Petteril near Southwaite, 8 miles from Broadmoor, was the home of William Holliday and Margaret Shaw's Aunt Jane, Mrs Holliday. They ran the mill and farmed its land in common with the adjacent stock farm, Petteril Bank Farm, for sixty years until 1897, when they put the Petteril Bank stock up for sale by auction. A sale bill in the possession of the family describes Mr Holliday as one of the oldest tenant farmers in the district, 'widely known as a very prominent breeder of Shorthorns, Clydesdale Horses and Swine'. His stock comprised 35 head of pure bred Shorthorned cattle; 121 Clydesdale horses; 117 sheep including Leicester ewes and border Leicester rams; 18 pigs; stocks of oats, wheat and rye; heaps of marigolds, swedes and potatoes; the usual farm implements and some surplus furniture. He retired to Barrow Mill, where another sale followed after his death in 1910. The livestock was then down to two milking cows, two heifers, a bullock and an old brown horse, but there was an interesting collection of domestic items including fifty pictures, a Chippendale candle stand, a Chippendale card table, feather beds, oak, walnut and mahogany furniture, and 'a very large host of other articles too numerous to particularize, being a total clearance of a very old Housekeeper'.

Mrs Holliday, Margaret Shaw's Aunt Jane.

Stephen Shaw (left) in a tub trap with Mr William Holliday at Barrow Mill. The barn has been much altered and the pig hull, now with much of its roof missing, awaits restoration.

William Holliday at Barrow Mill, 1905. The window with its chamfered frame has been replaced and the cobbles covered with tarmac.

Black and white leghorns and some Rhode Island Reds at Petteril Bank, 1905. Like many similar farmhouses on the fringe of the Lake District, it has been 'modernised' almost beyond recognition.

Clydesdale, Petteril Bank. At William Holliday's sale here in 1897 his eleven Clydesdales were variously described as 'good sort and regular Breeder', 'Prize Winner', 'very promising' and 'like making a powerful horse'.

Mole catching: Dick Osborne and dogs.

Lambing time. The house in the centre background is Langwath Farm on the road from Penrith to Wigton.

The harvest field.

Blackberry time: Miss Esther Graham and Dick Osborne.

Dick Osborne shows Billy Rooke how to cut a hedge stake. The picture was originally captioned 'Back end'.

The railwayman, 1905. At the peak of the railway's heyday in Britain, about 1910, nearly 170,000 people worked in stations as station-masters, ticket collectors, porters, signalmen, shunters and clerks. Railway work was arduous and dangerous. The Board of Trade reported that on a single day, 31 December 1901, 8,087 men worked more than eighteen hours. Between 1901 and 1911, 5,508 railwaymen were killed and 238,798 injured.

The General Railway Regulations in Britain in 1877 required that a candidate for porter should be not less than 5 feet 7 inches tall, aged 21 to 35, intelligent, fit, strong, able to read and write, and provided with three character references, one of them from his previous employer. Discipline was institutionalised in a system of cautions, fines and dismissals. A circular in 1872 listed a booking clerk dismissed for not accounting for excess fares, a booking clerk cautioned for erroneously booking a passenger through ignorance of the train service, a telegraph clerk fined for violently using his instrument, a ticket collector cautioned for incivility, a parcels porter dismissed for being absent without leave, and a porter fined for damaging a passenger's box. At a tiny British station, the station-master might be signalman, porter and booking clerk combined.

Postman at Broadmoor Farm, *c.* 1906. Wages and hours for country postmen seem to have been similar to those of farm labourers. The rates for London postmen are given in a handbill issued by the Postman's Union in 1890 for distribution outside South Kensington Museum where the Jubilee of Uniform Penny Post was being celebrated. A postman's wage was 18*s* a week at starting and all the parcel postmen in London, over 500 of them, were paid at this rate except for a few at 19*s*. Many postmen were employed for only five or six hours a day, earning only 9*s* to 13*s* a week. They were unable to get supplementary employment because these hours were spread over a fourteen- to sixteen-hour day. Over half the postmen in London were paid less than the rate for unskilled labour established by the dock workers. None of them got a decent wage until they had served over twelve or fifteen years, and hundreds continued at 16*s* or 18*s* all their lives.

Rural postmen covered long distances, and besides delivering letters and parcels acted as a kind of peripatetic post office, selling stamps, weighing parcels, accepting registered letters and obtaining postal orders for the immobile. They knew all that went on in their area and were usually welcome callers to farmers and especially their wives, isolated in remote hamlets.

Housemaid, Rosley House, 1902. Mrs Rooke is driving.

Pensioner, Causa Grange, Rosley, 1904. However hard a man worked during his active years, and however frugally he tried to save, there came a time when his earning powers diminished and, unless his family supported him, he was faced with the horror of the workhouse. For many old people, the most significant legislation of the century was the Old Age Pensions Act of 1908, which provided the over-seventies who were without means 5*s* a week, or 7*s* 6*d* a week for a married couple. As described by Flora Thompson, it transformed the life of villagers: 'They were relieved of anxiety. They were suddenly rich. Independent for life! At first, when they went to the Post Office to draw it, tears of gratitude would run down the cheeks of some, and they would say as they picked up their money, "God bless that Lloyd George . . . and God bless you, Miss" and there were flowers from their gardens and apples from their trees for the girl who merely handed them the money.'

Mary Ann Younghusband, retired landlady of the Wheatsheaf, 1901.

4

DOMESTIC LIFE

In the captions written on the boxes and envelopes of plates there are some forty personal names and twenty names of houses or places. Less than half of either can now be positively identified and the rest of the collection is, therefore, presented as elements in the life style of the various social groups and events of the period in Kendal and the Lakes.

Babies and small children were, as in all family albums, popular photographic subjects, the former appearing surrounded by adoring female relatives. Proud fathers are, however, conspicuously absent, less being expected then of middle-class men in this world of nurseries and nursemaids.

Baby worship: the Grays, 1908.

The christening gown, Lane Foot, Strickland Roger, now Windermere Road, Kendal. Bulmers' Directory for 1905 gives the occupant of Lane Foot as Percy Coulthard, farmer.

Mrs Loveday and twins, 1905.

Jane Quinn, a close friend of Margaret Shaw, and Theodora, 1912.

The enchanting feature of these early twentieth-century children is how happy they seem, even when posed for the camera. In the 1830s, middle-class adults enjoyed and petted their children and had them prettily dressed up in the evenings but, about the middle of the century, a draconian attitude to child education developed. Under the malign influence of Arnold of Rugby, children were brought up to fear God and their fathers in about equal proportions. They were satiated with intense religious training: daily family prayers, constant church going and the reading of interminable sermons on Sundays. Kept well out of sight of adults apart from a ceremonial visit downstairs before bed, their lives upstairs were constrained and austere.

In the 1870s some of the worst abuses of children were curbed by law; sending them up chimneys as sweeps was stopped in 1875, and the Acts of 1870 and 1876 introduced for the first time a system of elementary education for all. Employers in general believed that the working class would be less happy if educated but that perhaps they might be taught to read for the purpose of studying the scriptures. In 1900, when the first nursery school was opened, the event was described as heralding the dawn of 'the children's century', and in 1902 another Education Act gave county authorities responsibilities for secondary schools, primarily to provide capable manpower for industry and commerce. Despite its provisions, less than a fifth of Edwardian boys reached a secondary school of any kind, the others leaving school at twelve.

The children in the photographs dressed up as little Edwardian adults were no doubt constantly admonished not to get their clothes dirty. The little girl posed in a Kendal yard wears the traditional outfit for Easter Sunday, new bonnet with knee length ribbons, dress, gloves, shoes and socks in a light colour, in this case probably white, and a basket of daffodils tied with a big bow. Irene Green is sensibly attired for play, in an unironed smock, scuffed shoes and wrinkly stockings. Little Allan Green was fortunate to have been born just too late for the slaughter of the Great War.

The sailor frock, 1905.

The Easter outfit, Yard 127, Highgate, Kendal. The steps have gone, but the long window and the cobbles survive.

Irene and Allan Green, 1904.

Irene and Allan Green, 1904.

The toy horse: Billy Rooke, Rosley House. One of the widest class differences in Edwardian Britain was in the provision of toys. Working-class children were sent out to play and if they had any toys at all these would be adjuncts of street games – marbles and whips and tops for boys, skipping ropes for girls, hoops and balls for either. There are no photographs of children's nurseries in the collection but they would certainly have shown dolls' houses, rocking horses and tinplate mechanical toys. For playing in the garden we see in these photographs a doll's pram, two designs of doll's pushchair, several dolls, two toy horses and two tricycles. The sex roles are clear, as they are on p. 42 where the girl mends stockings while the boy reads the newspaper. Besides these simple toys, a dog was usually on hand for entertainment. Playing outside the garden with street children would have been unthinkable.

Billy Rooke and his tricycle, Rosley House.

Irene and Allan Green, 1904. Allan's horse has been reharnessed.

The doll's pram.

The Middleton twins, 1902.

Prince and friend at home at 157 Stricklandgate. Prince was buried at no. 157, his headstone being eventually removed to the churchyard across the road by a later occupant of the house.

Studies on rabies in nineteenth-century dogs have shown that dogs and dog fanciers increased steadily in numbers in late Victorian times. Working-class dogs were kept for poaching, racing and farm work and, in those homes that could afford to feed them, as pets.

The middle-class dogs shown here served no doubt for house security, as companions to the young and elderly or as dress accessories. Notwithstanding the exaggerated claims made for cats as eradicators of vermin, they were usually kept as women's and children's pets and as a kind of stage property, helping to create a domestic idyll of hearth and home.

Town dog, with Mrs Witt at heel. The house in Aglionby Street, Carlisle, was owned by Edward Bewley of Rosley, brother of Margaret Shaw's husband.

Country dogs at Causa Grange, Rosley, *c.* 1902.

Mrs Charles Fildes, daughters and cat taking tea at Overdale, Kendal Green, 1905.

Art nouveau was the perfect background for the genteel life and, like the reproduction styles of furnishing and decor, the provinces got it second-hand. By the time the movement reached England from France, the steam had run out of it. In Britain it centred around Liberty's in Regent Street, Goodyer's and Storey and Co. Supporters of the style found in it beauty of line, grace of form and freedom; critics described it as the concentrated essence of wriggle, as abounding in squirming lines and blobs, as a conscious striving after novelty, as decadent and nonsensical and as fidgetily vulgar and obtrusive. Voysey thought it demonstrated atheism, conceit and imitation.

None of these opinions obstructed art nouveau's commercial acceptance, and the wallpapers and furnishings of these interiors show motifs of lilies, poppies and other 'decadent' plants grafted in amongst William Morris, Arts and Crafts designs and the accretions of preceding Victorians.

This photograph shows Mrs Stephen Shaw – and a typical interior of the time – at 157 Stricklandgate in 1905.

Malcolm Shaw, 157 Stricklandgate.

Tea room. The picture at top right is a reproduction of a Romney portrait of Bishop Law, the lower right and perhaps some of the others are of Romney's Emma Hart (Lady Hamilton). Perhaps this is the interior of the Tivoli Tea Room a few doors south of Redman's Yard, Kendal, where George Romney was an apprentice. Margaret Shaw seems to have enjoyed cafés and, according to her diaries, took tea at the Ferry Hotel on Windermere, at 'Staggs' in Bowness, at the Emperor Café, Carlisle, at Reece's and the Edinburgh Café in Liverpool, at Rowntrees in Southport and at Tilly's in Newcastle.

The Victorian architect, Robert Kerr, in his comprehensive book *The Gentleman's House* (1864), gave affluent nineteenth-century industrialists aspiring to gentry status some useful hints on decoration and furniture. Dining room furniture should be massive and simple in keeping with English fare; long lines of chairs ranged along the walls make a room look like a tavern; elegance may be brought to a drawing room by introducing chairs and couches, occasional tables, sofa tables, pier tables, chiffoniers, fancy cabinets, what-nots and a cabinet pianoforte. Fifty years later these ideas had filtered down the social scale to the middle classes. In the drawing rooms of these Cumbrian housewives, the simple, robust, functional and sparse furnishings of their yeoman forefathers have given way to factory furniture vulgarised for a mass market. On p. 25 we see the traditional settle; here is its Edwardian sequel, the settee.

The sofa – the Arabic soffah after two centuries of naturalisation. The art nouveau poppy-pattern wallpaper contrasts with the traditional floral carpet and the beadwork footstool.

The pianoforte, Westward Parks, near Wigton, 1906. Sir Laurence Alma-Tadema had recently raised the decoration of pianos to new heights with a Broadwood inlaid with coloured woods 'combined with ivory, brass and alabaster, in a rich Byzantine design'.

Bessie Watson, farmer, with her Victorian china cabinet, successor to the medieval court cupboard or buffet. Displaying the best china signified wealth and status.

The universal popularity of gardening in the Lake Counties in the Edwardian era is attested by the numbers of nurserymen and seedsmen recorded in the trade directories. Excluding agricultural seedsmen, there were in Kelly's Directory for 1906 no fewer than eighteen in Carlisle, many of them with their nursery gardens in nearby villages, four in Penrith and sixteen others distributed between nine other Cumberland towns. Westmorland had ten, distributed between seven towns. Working-class gardens were for food production, middle-class gardens for status, recreation and the kitchen.

The bigger gardens shown here display prestigious cedars, providing shade for summer tea parties, and the novelty Monkey Puzzle, introduced from Chile by William Lobb in the 1840s (seen here at Rosley House in 1905). Virginia creeper, Clematis and climbing roses decorate the house and garden walls, urns of geraniums flank the doorways and rustic plantaria, garden seats, deck chairs, garden tents and tennis nets variously adorn the lawns and drives.

Flower borders are either long rectangles or follow the curving sweep of an entrance drive. Planted for colour and seasonal effect, almost all show some influence of Gertrude Jekyll, though rarely so softly coloured or gently textured. The herbaceous plants are the old traditional garden flowers: asters, Canterbury bells, dahlias, delphiniums, nasturtiums, Michaelmas daisies, phlox, sweet peas and tiger lilies.

Webster Cottage, 1910. The location is unknown but the window surrounds suggest north Cumberland. Roses, dahlias, chrysanthemums, Michaelmas daisies and perhaps Solomon's Seal dominate this autumn garden.

Orphan Cragg ('Miss Collinson's cottage'), Underbarrow, 1905. The road is now tarmacked, the cobbles have gone, the windows have been replaced and the barn on the left has been converted to a house. This autumn photograph shows ivy, roses and clematis climbing the wall and lilies, fern and perhaps candytuft filling the raised border.

Architect's garden. Irene and Allen Green and Prince in the front garden of 157 Stricklandgate. It appears to have been laid out on a drawing board.

'The Runner Bean': the end of the kitchen garden at Underwood, overlooking Kendal Fell.

A rustic plantarium and Eleanor Rooke, Rosley House, *c.* 1907.

Garden urns. Billy Rooke is posing with his tricycle outside Rosley House, *c.* 1907.

Garden seat: art nouveau at Underwood, Queen's Road, Kendal, 1902.

Flowers for the house, *c.* 1906.

Mr and Miss Stevenson gathering a posy, 1905.

Flowers for the guests: Mrs Rooke and Billy at Rosley House, 1909. The guests are Mr J.F.W. Ritson, the family solicitor, and May Sharpe.

Folding garden shelter. Mr Brunskill and family, Underwood.

In the early 1900s, when cars were still costly toys rather than a serious form of transport, a smart turnout with high-stepping horses, a coachman and an elegant hand-built carriage was the prestigious status symbol occupied by the chauffeur-driven car of a later date. Carriages were of many sorts – victorias, phaetons, landaus – descending in status to broughams, governess carts, traps and gigs of the humblest and shabbiest sorts. Margaret Shaw's photographs show horse-drawn vehicles of many sorts from the Middleton's victoria to the Broadmoor farm cart, seen here outside Sandy Brow smithy, Rosley. The traditional two-wheeled farm cart, in use all over Britain, was of a size and construction to match the strength of the average farm draught horse. Its wide wheel hoops allowed it to pass over all but the softest ground with a heavy load of turnips or even stones. For a light material such as hay it would be extended with inward sloping sideboards and shelvings, frames extending forwards over the horse and backwards. The cart was balanced to be easily tipped on the release of a catch and the wheels were 'dished': that is, the hub was set in from the plane of the rim so that the wheel slanted outwards at the top to clear the body of the cart, while the spokes taking the thrust to the ground were vertical.

The trap, Broadmoor, *c.* 1906. The trap, sprung and high off the ground to reduce the downward drag on the horse, is built for lightness. The form of the wheels strictly follows the lines of force, and the outer edges of the spokes and of the fellowes between the spokes which are not load-bearing are pared away to reduce the weight.

The barn behind the trap is much altered now and the little pig hull is semi-derelict.

Malcolm Shaw, Easter 1903. The vehicle is a type of dog cart known as an alexandra, a battlesden car or a moray car. The let-down footboard at the rear enabled one or two passengers to sit back-to-back with the 'whip' (driver). Two-wheeled dog carts needed movable seats or sliding bodies to get the correct balance for the horse according to the number of people on board.

Tradesman's delivery cart. The Hawkshead greengrocer at Gillbank, the Fildes family home at Colt House, 1908.

The wagonette. Malcolm Shaw driving with Billy, Mrs Rooke and duenna, 1909. Early versions of this vehicle were made for Lord Curzon in 1842 and, to the specifications of the Prince Consort, for Queen Victoria in 1845. With seats on both sides and, in this version, a box for driver and front seat for passenger, it was useful as a station wagon and luggage cart and also for picnics and sightseeing. It could be driven either to a pair or a single horse.

The pony phaeton. Misses Brunskill at Underwood, Queen's Road, Kendal, 1904. Phaetons, first popular in the 1780s, went out of fashion in the early nineteenth century, but were revived by George IV when he became too stout to drive a more sporting vehicle. The great advantage of the pony phaeton to the stout and elderly, and also to ladies with voluminous skirts, was that the bodywork was low slung with the mounting step only a few inches above the ground. The model shown here is a vis-à-vis type for four people.

The victoria. Mr and Mrs Middleton, the twins and coachman outside 157 Stricklandgate, 1905. The victoria, an English version of an elegant coachman-driven vehicle used in Paris, was named after Queen Victoria who, like Edward VII, then Prince of Wales, greatly admired it. It was fashionable until the 1900s, partly because of royal patronage and partly because the absence of doors allowed a becoming display of the ladies' skirts. The model seen here is a panel-boot victoria with a single folding seat behind the box-seat.

The picnic-drive. Mrs Shaw, Malcolm, Margaret and Prince with Mrs Rooke near Rosley Common, 1902. The vehicle is a spindled-back Siamese phaeton, with two identical seats one behind the other.

5

FASHION

Edwardian ladies spent a great deal of time dressing and undressing. There were simple costumes for morning errands and more ornate ones for morning visits, besides luncheon frocks, afternoon gowns, walking dresses, gowns for visiting and gowns for family gatherings, for official ceremonies, for lectures and sermons, for dinner parties, concerts or balls, for the races, motor car trips, train journeys, sea voyages and visits to the seaside and mountains, all identified by 'Vogue' and 'Harper's Bazaar'.

The characteristic feature of the era was the Gibson Girl style, an S-shape with a large bosom, small waist and ample posterior. Until about 1910 dresses were usually in two pieces, a bodice or blouse and a skirt. Following the fashion set by Queen Alexandra, bodices and blouses were generally high necked, belts were tightened to narrow the waist and skirts were padded at the back. Summer dresses achieved the fashionable female silhouette with bodices loaded with frills and flounces, a constricted waist and ground length skirts, sometimes filled out by pleats. Waist lines started to rise in 1907 and fell again in the 1920s, to hip level in 1925.

For fashionable women there was a revolution in underwear, the functional garments of Victoria's reign being replaced by lingerie, openly advertised as seductive. Drawers were replaced by knickers, the shift evolved through the chemise to the slip and petticoats became frilly. The most sensational new garment, the brassière, was introduced in 1912, the preceding cult of the bust being attained by judicious lacing.

In the photographs we see only daytime wear, mainly afternoon tea gowns, with the extreme styles of Knightsbridge muted to those of sensible Kendal.

Afternoon wear. Tea group at Underwood, Kendal, 1908.

Two-piece suit. The English tailor-made, originated by Charles Worth for the Empress Eugénie and produced for women generally by the French designer, Doucet, became very popular. The wearer, Margaret Shaw's friend Jane Quinn, seen here outside 157 Stricklandgate, appears to be ready for church with psalter and hymn book under her arm.

Walking dress. Millie Sharpe of Laurel Bank, Castle Road, Kendal.

Fur and feathers. Margaret Shaw and the Sharpe sisters outside Windermere Grammar School, Easter 1905. May Sharpe has an astrakhan muff, Gertie a fox fur, Fannie a reversible silk-lined astrakhan stole and Margaret Shaw a feather boa. The school, opened in 1885, was demolished in 1965.

Man about town. Mr Drewser outside 157 Stricklandgate, 1903. Edward VII led fashion in the early 1900s by wearing lounge suits instead of frock coats, and the homburg which he brought back from Germany. With the invention of the trouser press in the 1890s creases moved from the sides to the front and back, and turn-ups became fashionable for lounge suits. With this outfit Mr Drewser sports a thorn walking stick with silver mountings and a fob watch with chain. His waistcoat, square-cut at the bottom, is double breasted and has the bottom buttons fastened. The fashion for leaving the bottom button undone, still practised, began in 1908.

'The time has come, designers say, to talk of many things, of shoes and furs and lingerie and if one flares or clings, and where the waistline ought to be and whether hats have wings.' Gwen Raverat describes her aunt buying a hat in Regent Street towards the end of the century: 'a little black and gold-braided bonnet with four yellow roses and a little narrow black velvet ribbon'. For this succulent little number she paid £2. By 1900, however, bonnets were being replaced by hats and the Edwardian cartwheel hat was on its way. Summer hats were commonly of straw, leghorn or a variety of other materials such as crin, lace or tulle, with wide brims profusely ornamented with flowers, feathers, plumes, ribbons and tulle or chiffon drapery. Those shown here were photographed at a tea party on Kendal Golf Links in 1907.

The same occasion. The hat worn by the lady on the left has the narrower brim and high, lavishly decorated crown popular in 1907.

More tea on the Golf Links, 1907. Golfing hats made in eight pieces and hats like meringues were also popular. The medieval style of the hat worn by the older woman shows the influence of the aesthetic movement.

The Sunday hat, 1901.

The Middleton twins, 1902.

Elph Howe, Kentmere, 1908. The sun hats, worn for the garden, are of traditional design.

'There was an Old Man with a beard
Who said, 'It is just as I feared –
Two Owls and a Hen, four Larks and a Wren,
Have all built their nests in my beard!'
Edward Lear, 1846

In Victorian times, immense soft, silky beards were regarded as irresistible. The styles of beards sported in the early 1900s ranged with decreasing age of the wearer from the patriarchal, as demonstrated by Uncle Edward's, through the Rasputin style and the Old Sea Dog's fringe to the smartly trimmed and pointed type favoured by Edward VII.

Uncle Edward (left), born in 1832, was photographed in 1908. His frock coat and wide-lapelled double-breasted waistcoat belong to the 1890s. On the right is Mr Armstrong, joiner and innkeeper at Curthwaite, 1901.

Mr Witt, 1902.

Mrs Wright in her bath chair taking the air, 1904. Queen Victoria died in 1901 having been on the throne throughout the adult life of Mrs Wright, and also Aunt Ann and Aunt Ettie overleaf. These costumes show many features of the Old Queen's style – the black she wore consistently after the death of Albert, richly brocaded bombazines and silks, black gloves, black hats and a few touches of jet in hatpins and buttons.

'Aunt Ann and Aunt Ettie'. Aunt Ann (left) wears a coat trimmed with white scalloped decoration at the shoulders and an art nouveau design at the cuffs in white braid. Below the waist it is filled out with pleats. A veil and black and white ostrich feathers decorate her hat and the outfit is completed by a long feather boa.

6

The Social Round

Tea as a meal was regarded in Victorian and Edwardian times as a most useful form of easy and cheap entertaining, Mrs Beeton remarking that a great many guests may be welcomed to an afternoon tea at a cost that can scarce be reckoned. At a regular 'At Home', given every week or every month, small cups and no plates were provided and only tea, thin bread and butter and cakes were expected. For an 'At Home' on a specific date, there would be such things as ices, claret and champagne cup, small fancy sandwiches such as *foie gras* or cucumber and a great variety of small sweets.

High teas were regarded as especially convenient for summer when out-door amusements might be going on and guests could be invited and served informally. Mrs Beeton suggests a summer 'High Tea' menu of 'Mayonnaise of Salmon, Cold Chicken, Tongue, Galantine of Veal, Salad, Cucumber, Compote of Fruit, Jelly, Pound Cake, Strawberries and Cream, Tea, Coffee, etc.'

Afternoon tea occupies much of the diaries of Margaret Shaw who, if she was well and not away from Kendal, entertained guests for tea, dinner or supper about three times a week. Tea parties were about twice as frequent as dinner and supper parties together, the guests arriving for tea usually about four o'clock and leaving sometimes as late as ten or eleven o'clock, supper having also been served.

Maggie went out to tea or supper about as often as she entertained, her circle of tea party friends, as indicated by her diaries, extending to about fifty families, couples or individuals. From the evidence of the photographs, tea as served by frugal Kendalians was not quite as lavish as recommended by Mrs Beeton, and guests scraped by on one or two plates of sandwiches, currant buns or scones, parkin, a sandwich cake and some fancy cakes.

Tea at Lane Foot, Kendal, 1911. Chromium plate, as seen on the sandwich basket and the cake stand, is typical of this period as also are the spindly legs of the tables. So too are the gentleman's side parting, a style dating from about 1905; the large waxed moustache, rarely seen after the Great War; and the cigarette. Improvements in cultivation and processing of tobacco early in the century made the smoke less acid and easier to inhale, and brought a major expansion in cigarette smoking. Prejudice against women smoking was not broken until the Great War.

Tea with Miss Collinson, Orphan Cragg, Underbarrow, 1905. The room shows the influence of the aesthetic movement – wild flowers on the table, blue and white china on the panelling and on the bookcase, the swirl of the design on the damask tablecloth. The rusticity of the seventeenth century has been enhanced by a sophisticated taste. Today the panelling and the flagged floor have gone and the exterior is much altered (see p. 58, lower picture).

Tea tables of this type with four hinged flaps and a shelf were particularly recommended by Mrs Beeton for the space they provided. In this model the books were perhaps needed for stability rather than for ready reference.

Tea at Lane Foot, Kendal. The spirit lamp under the tea kettle served to keep the water warm for the teapot. The 'key' pattern on the tablecloth, Egyptian in origin, reflects the popularity of Egyptology following the excavations by Sir Flinders Petrie from 1881 onwards. Note the mass of tablecloths, traycloths, doilies and mats in linen, lace and crochet work.

Tea at Underwood, Kendal. When central heating was rare and houses were often cold and damp, rheumatism was a common affliction of the elderly. Great importance was attached to not sitting on damp grass and here mats and footstools have been provided to avoid it. Beside the cat's saucer a bell is at hand to summon a housemaid with fresh supplies for the teatable.

Afternoon tea was a device to occupy middle-class women with time to kill, and 'tea groups' form by far the largest subject in this collection. Men appear infrequently in the tea group photographs and those that do often look bored and frustrated. This tea group was photographed at Laurel Bank, Castle Road, Kendal, in 1911. Mr Thomas Sharpe (front row), bootmaker of Atkinson and Sharpe, would like everyone to go home.

Picnic at Strawberry Gardens, 1908. The couple on the right have brought their tea in a carrier bag from Miss E. Lishman, confectioner of Victoria Street, Windermere. The other carrier bag, 'Flavour wins favour', is from Thomas Leighton and Son, Grocers of 48 Highgate, Kendal. A matrimonial row appears to be brewing between the couple in front of the cedar trunk.

Nothing could be further from the '*déjeuner sur l'herbe*' of the French Impressionists than these photographs of afternoon picnics in Westmorland. Custom and climate combine to dictate full-length skirts, blouses and hats for the women and waistcoats, hats and four-inch collars for the men. This is Gertie Sisson's picnic. Chairs, stools and rugs have been brought along for the ladies while the men chivalrously sit on the grass.

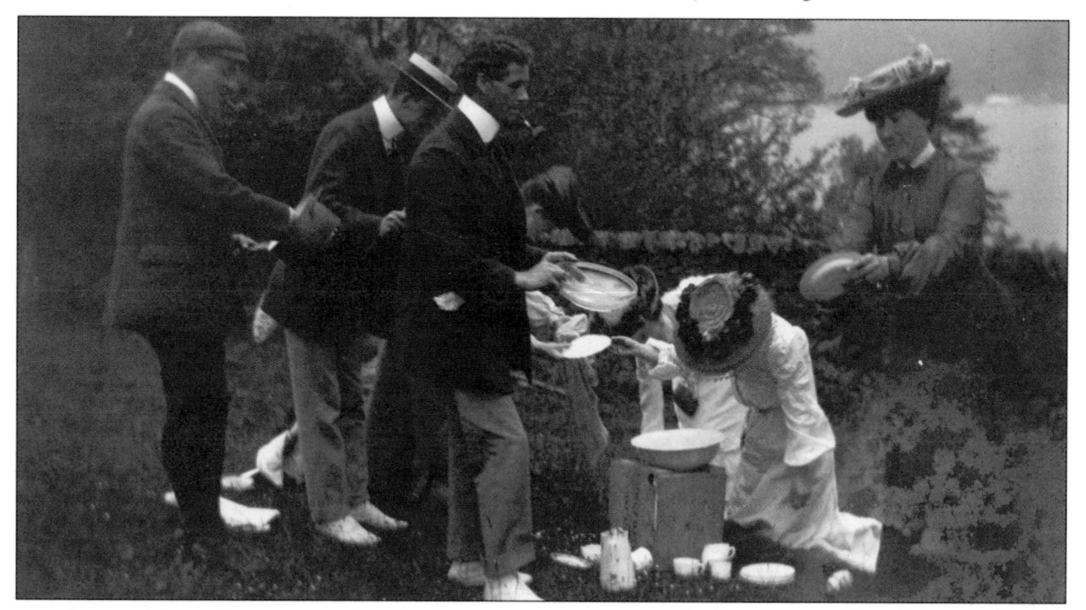

Mr Drewser's picnic, 1904. Two of the young men are wearing blazers, a word which first came into the language in 1880. They show an American influence with the broad cut and wide arm holes allowing freedom of movement. The grey flannels have turn-ups and are worn with fashionable, white canvas, rubber-soled shoes. Harry Lyon on the left wears a country outfit of tweed Norfolk jacket, breeches and stockings and a close-fitting tweed cap.

The Stevensons' picnic, Lake Windermere, 1906. Mr Stevenson is pictured with kettle, teapot, six ladies and six baskets of picnic tea.

Windermere picnic, 1907. Malcolm Shaw is washing the teapot.

On 7 September 1910, James Winstanley Cropper married Marjorie Constance Bagot, second daughter of Captain Bagot MP, and Mrs Bagot of Levens Hall, at Heversham Church. Nearly all the county families were represented. After the service, Mr Cropper's Ulverston troop of yeomanry formed a triumphal arch of drawn swords outside the church, the schoolchildren forming an arch of white flowers. A reception for the numerous friends of both families was held in Levens Hall; the employees and tenants of the Cropper family who had been brought in a charabanc from Burneside and the villagers from Levens had tea in a marquee on the lawn.

In a comprehensive account of the wedding, the *Westmorland Gazette* devoted eleven column inches to the families, the guests, the service, the music, the reception, the best man and what the bride and six bridesmaids wore, and thirty-six column inches to the wedding presents and their donors. The latter ranged from sundry viscounts, knights and ladies to the household servants, the schoolchildren and Miss Bagot's bible class. The presents were itemised in separate lists for the bridegroom and bride. He received 171 presents, which included nine cheques. She did rather better with 206 presents, only two cheques but also a diamond necklace, a diamond ring, a diamond brooch, a diamond bracelet, a diamond hair ornament and about thirty assorted brooches, bracelets, pendants, rings, chains, buckles and pins in various combinations of gold, diamonds, amethysts, emeralds, pearls, sapphires and opals.

There was a certain amount of duplication in the other presents which included, *inter alia*, forty pieces of furniture, his mainly old oak, hers mainly Chippendale; thirty-two books or sets of books including the complete works of Ruskin, Thackeray and R.L. Stevenson; twenty-four assorted trays and salvers; twenty-three pictures or groups of pictures including oils, watercolours and prints; eighteen travelling cases, dressing cases, dispatch boxes and similar ware; fourteen assorted vases and pairs of vases; twelve inkstands and inkpots; eleven Chippendale and other mirrors; nine assorted cruets, salt, pepper and mustard pots; seven clocks; six umbrellas; five pairs of silver candlesticks; three silver tea sets; three whips; two cigar lighters; two Thermos flasks, advertised in the early 1900s as an essential accompaniment for outdoor occupations; a saddle, a barometer and a fire extinguisher.

This photograph shows the bride and her father, Captain Josceline Bagot. Following the fashion introduced by Queen Victoria, the bride wears a white wedding dress with veil and bouquet of white lilies. Little girls scatter daisies in the path of the bride.

On 29 June 1904, Maisie Cropper, daughter of the Burneside paper-mill owners, married Walter Morley Fletcher, a rising Cambridge physiologist. The *Westmorland Gazette's* reporter excelled himself in describing the day – 'a delightful day of rosy-girdled June, when the calm air seemed full of hope and happiness. Seldom', he thought, 'had the midsummer sun smiled upon a fairer bride.' The Cropper wedding did even better than the Bagot wedding with thirteen column inches describing the wedding and the guests. The titles included a Knight and four Ladies, three Honourables, a Canon, no less than fifteen brace of Reverends and their wives, and a mixed bag of minor academic and military gents. The presents and their donors were listed in a mere thirteen column inches but nevertheless included a quantity of silver engraved with Latin tags from the groom's college friends, a pair of Constables and a number of useful items, including a lawnmower, a case of tools and again a fire extinguisher.

The villagers shown here are awaiting the wedding party outside Burneside Church. The approach has been garlanded with swags of paper from the paper-mill.

Bride and groom leaving the church between ranks of villagers and mill employees.

The bridesmaids. Their dresses were pink and blue figured Liberty net over white silk with pink belts, worn with pink straw hats with green wreaths, and bouquets of pink roses.

Burnside *en fête* as the wedding couple departs.

Hannah Graham, friend of Maggie Shaw since their schooldays, married fellow-Kendalian George French at St Thomas's church. After the wedding breakfast the couple left for their honeymoon in Edinburgh, and the wedding party went for a charabanc drive. The bride wore a contemporary wedding outfit of white tailor-made costume and matching white hat, her father sporting the short beard popularised by Edward VII and the formal silk hat of the previous century.

The presents. They included a silver tea service from the Working Men's Association where the bride had conducted the music class for a number of years, a silver mounted salad bowl from the members of St Thomas's choir, and a silver butter dish from the men of St Thomas's night school. The circular mirror could have been made by the Keswick School of Industrial Arts.

The wedding carriage ready for the newly weds with a sprig of lucky heather tucked under the bride's trousseau trunk. The vehicle is a clarence, named after the Duke of Clarence, later William IV. Originally a family conveyance seating four and driven from the box, it was introduced by an Oxford Street firm in about 1842. Discarded clarences were often used as cabs, the precursor of the London 'growler'.

'Hannah's drive'. The charabanc, a French version of the wagonette, was mainly used for shooting parties and other country house events. It had cross seats for seven including the driver, with a groom's seat at the rear. Later versions were fitted with extra seating for school parties and works outings. Here, eleven of Hannah's wedding guests have squeezed aboard and the horses are being driven 'unicorn' style. A charabanc of this type, manufactured by the Windermere Garage Co., survives at the carriage museum at Aysgarth Falls.

Counting the gate at the Garden Sale, 18 July 1907. A short newspaper report of this event records that it was held in the garden of Rosemont, Burneside Road, Kendal, overlooking Dockwray Hall mill on the River Kent. It raised £40 for the St John's Presbyterian church, built on Sandes Avenue ten years earlier.

The Rev. M.N.G. Gray in charge of the stall. The lady in black is perhaps Mrs Bryce of Burneside, who opened the sale.

Sale of Work. The lady to the left of the punter with the purchase shows the fashion in hats at this date, worn tipped forward and decorated at the back under the brim. She carries a parasol and an early design of handbag, evolved from the Victorian reticule.

Kendal's Home Nursing Association employed a permanent nurse to attend the sick poor of the town in their own homes at a salary of £75 a year. To provide a salary of £40 for an assistant nurse, needed in the winter months, the Association set out to raise money at a fête and bicycle gymkhana held in the ground of Abbot Hall on 12 July 1900. Mrs Bagot, newly returned from nursing the troops in the Boer War, opened the proceedings, observing that the nurses had paid nearly 3,000 visits in Kendal within the last year, and that the Association was in no way pauperising as all who could afford it were expected to pay for their own dressings and appliances. In proposing a vote of thanks of typical Edwardian obsequiousness, the Deputy Mayor, referring to her South African service, remarked that it would have been worth being hit by a Mauser bullet to have her kind words and nursing. The platform was then taken over by the Bijou orchestra which played while tea was served from a marquee and, with the Zingari Quartet and the Parish Church District Choir, presented three concerts during the day. An amateur dramatic society put on a comic charade in the Hall entitled 'Midnight', Malcolm Shaw playing the hero of the piece. According to the *Westmorland Gazette's* reporter it was not remarkable for its plot and was presented with some difficulty, the scenery and stage effects having been lost in transit.

This photograph shows the parasol parade. The *Gazette* report describes 'Sipping American drinks and disposing of ices in a tropical temperature.'

The highlight of the day, however, was the bicycle gymkhana. Twenty young ladies competed, dressed in white costumes and white straw hats with tri-coloured band. Each had a tri-coloured band worn bandalero fashion, a bell attached to an arm band and crossed Union Jacks on their handlebars. Accompanied by the Volunteer Band they started with a twelve-minute musical ride which included 2 miles of maze threading and other intricate manoeuvres. In the first race the competitors rode across the park, dismounted, threaded a needle held by a waiting gentleman, and raced back again. In the next, a poster had to be pasted and stuck on to a board at the half-way point. Others included a potato race with potatoes to be dropped into buckets, a mounted egg and spoon race and a donkey race in which the slowest rider won. Here we see the musical ride. Over the park wall is Jennings' Yard, and in the background the Town Hall clocktower and the carpet factory chimney.

The event was a great success and raised £115.

The platform party. Beneath a string of Chinese lanterns, Mr John Wakefield calls for three cheers for Mrs Bagot.

Tea in the park, set out on little tables and served by the ladies of the committee.

The Guild Drive to Patterdale, 1904. Church Guilds were popular institutions in the Edwardian era for integrating young people into church communities. Aimed at young adults between Sunday School age and young marrieds in their early thirties, they organised social events of which the annual guild excursion was the highlight. The photographs are of the Young People's Guild of St John's Presbyterian church in Sandes Avenue, Kendal, which had outings to Coniston in 1903 and Patterdale in 1904.

The group photograph. Stephen Shaw can be seen in the centre of the group, and the minister in boater and clerical collar on the front row.

Tea with the faithful. The minister with the magnificent moustache is the Rev. M.N.G. Gray, seen on p. 100 in his clerical hat.

The growing popularity of Grasmere Sports, begun in about 1880, is mirrored in the county directories and guide books. For example: 'Athletic sports held annually on the Thursday nearest 20th August' (Bulmer's Directory, 1885); 'The Grasmere and Lake District athletic sports are held annually under the patronage of almost the whole of the county gentry and comprise various north country amusements for which valuable prizes are offered' (Kelly's Directory, 1894); 'Great numbers of people assemble to witness the wrestling, pole leaping, tug of war and the exciting fell race and hound trail, etc. for the successful competitors of which prizes are offered' (Bulmer's Directory, 1905); 'The major Lakeland sporting event and by far the most popular in the area with up to 20,000 spectators. . . . A brilliant location with all the usual running, throwing and cycling events, attracting professionals from all over the country, along with the best of the traditional local events, such as Cumberland and Westmorland Wrestling. . . . Also the famous guides' fell race and hound trailing. . . . Full of atmosphere and excitement' (*The Good Guide*, Hunter Davies, 1984).

The spectators in the 1905 photograph, apparently gazing intently at nothing in particular, are perhaps waiting for the trail hounds to reappear in sight. At this date the natives occupied wooden benches around the wrestling ring while the gentry sat in their carriages in a double or triple ring around the perimeter.

The walkers in these photographs give the impression of having strolled along the road a short way from a trap or charabanc to admire the scenery, and the ladies in their big Edwardian hats are certainly not dressed for the fells. Maggie's diary for 1912 records walking from Kendal with Malcolm Shaw and their friends Harry and May Lyon to Sad Gill in Longsleddale. They stayed at the Fishwicks' and walked on to Mardale next day.

In the photograph Harry Lyon wears a clerical version of the young man's walking gear, Maggie in the boater has a feminine version of shirt, collar and tie. May Lyon on the left makes no concession to sporting styles. The photograph (dating from 1912) illustrates the care taken to place such groups in a well-balanced composition.

The road from Buttermere to Braithwaite with Keskadale Beck or Newlands Beck in the valley bottom, 1907. The Stevenson family has transport at a discreet distance behind.

Mr Drewser on the Ambleside to Keswick road modelling the correct attire for gentlemen in the country – Norfolk jacket, breeches, socks, collar and tie, and boater.

Gateway to the Lakes.

Proto-cyclist: Mrs Rooke learning to ride on the croquet lawn at Rosley, 1906.

Although the 'boneshaker' bicycle of wood and iron was invented in 1867, cycling as a popular amusement of the well-to-do dates from about 1890, when the pneumatic tyre provided a comfort previously lacking. When the cycling vogue began, bicycles were treated much as if they had been horses. A lady planning a ride in Regent's Park would have the machine sent in the charge of a footman, travel there in her own carriage, ride round and round on the smooth roads and return as she had come.

By 1900, cycling had spread down the social scale and membership of the Cyclists Touring Club reached 60,000. Mixed cycling in clubs provoked public cries of alarm at the prospect of moral chaos as daughters escaped unchaperoned to meet members of the opposite sex.

From 1901, Baddeley's famous *Thorough Guide* to the English Lake District included a section for cyclists with a warning that 'it is not a county to ride through without a brake'. Noting the unyielding nature of stone walls, it recommended readers not to ride down Kirkstone Pass, Graythwaite Hill, the direct descent from Windermere to Keswick or the 'break-neck' Red Bank to Grasmere. The bicycles in the photographs have either no brake or one which operated by pressing down on the front tyre.

Kick start. An experienced rider demonstrates the technique of mounting from behind the bike with a foot on the back step. The onlookers are outside St Thomas's church, Kendal, after a morning service.

Cyclist, *c.* 1905. The chain shield and several hatpins make this costume practical. The location is outside 157 Stricklandgate, Kendal, at the foot of House of Correction Hill. The building on the right is the Wesleyan Chapel.

The Stevenson sisters, 1906, nicknamed by Margaret Shaw 'The Stevenettes'. Her diary records Mrs Stevenson, Robin, Janet and various animals leaving for Ardrossan from Oxenholme at Easter 1912, Mr Stevenson staying on with the Shaws to say his last goodbyes.

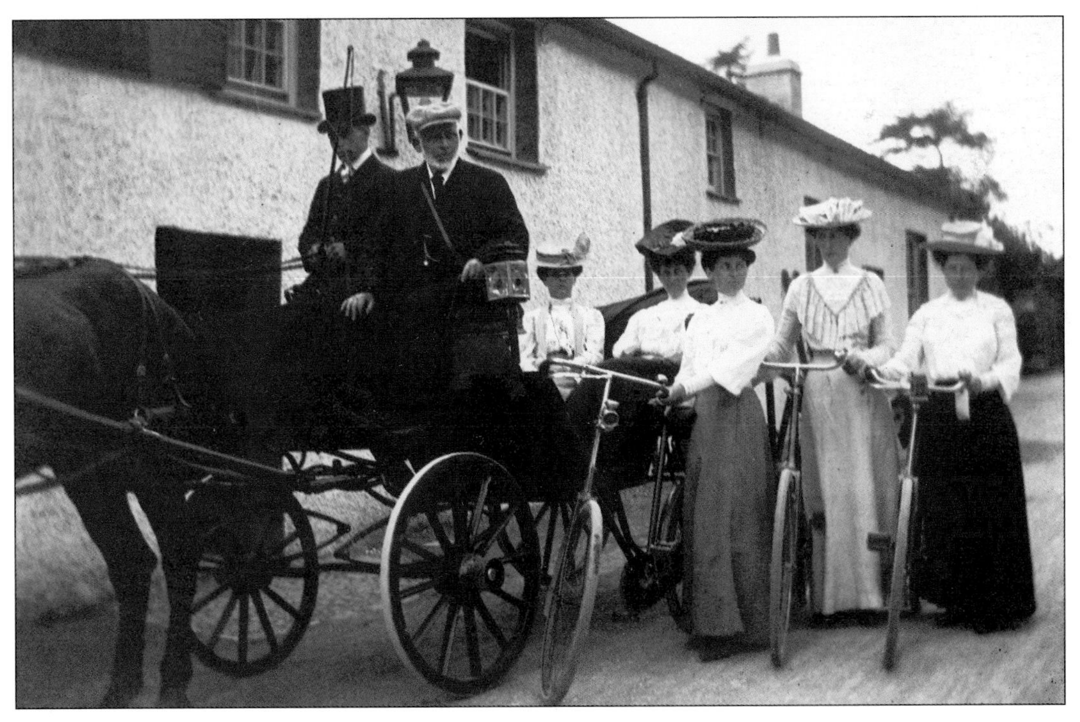

The Stevenettes outside the Nag's Head, Wythburn, 1906.

The Stevenettes outside Kentmere church, 1906. Note the luggage label on the bicycle on the right. The range for cyclists was greatly increased by a good railway service with stops at numerous tiny stations. Bicycles could be stowed in the luggage van and retrieved at a station near the destination, in this case no doubt Staveley station.

The idea of camping as an escape from urban civilisation was well established in Edwardian days. Good care was taken to mitigate the rigours of the simple life under canvas by bringing along deck chairs, a trestle table and quantities of kitchen ware. The standards of comfort were perhaps acquired from those who had first-hand experience of camp life in the Indian Empire, where the supply of servants was unlimited.

From the site shown here, the campers could look out over Windermere while reclining supported on one elbow.

This meal was certainly not cooked on site. The men seem to have done the camping while the women ferried out large supplies of home-cooked food. The scene is framed in concentric rings of fungus, which attacked the emulsion when the plate was damp.

Stephen Shaw, Malcolm and friends at breakfast. With boiled eggs, pork pies and a pile of toast the party seems well provisioned.

'Surprise Party at Camp, May 21st, 1903.'

Proto-tennis, 1906: the transition to tennis from battledore and shuttlecock. Lawn tennis became the fashionable game for country-house parties in the 1880s, displacing croquet in popularity. Tennis had formerly been played only on walled and roofed courts, but in 1874 Major Walter Wingfield patented a new and improved portable court which allowed the game to be played on lawns. The Lawn Tennis Association was founded in 1886. A generation later the game had filtered down the social ladder to become a popular pastime of the middle classes.

Tea interval: the tennis court at the Ferry Hotel, Windermere, 1906. Onlookers on the terrace are protected from stray shots by netting fixed between tall poles.

Tennis trio. May, Gertie and Millie Sharpe of Laurel Bank, Kendal, *c.* 1904. Tennis clothes were usually white linen and consisted of dress or skirt and blouse, the skirts reaching to just above the ankles. No concessions were made to practicality until the 1920s when shorter, more functional, tennis outfits were accepted. These girls in their high-necked dresses with long sleeves and full skirts must have found the game hot. Millie Sharpe on the right holds a 'Demon' racket with the butt shaped like a demon's horns, a design in use from about 1895 to 1910. The racket on the left is typical of the shapes in vogue from the 1880s to the 1890s. The construction behind the players appears to be an artificial grotto in the rustic taste.

Kendal golf course, 1906. This course, on former common grazing land, dates as an eighteen-hole course from about 1897 when a pre-existing nine-hole club acquired a lease of 88 acres on Kendal Fell. The photograph shows the second green, with the top of Serpentine Woods in the background and Benson Knott in the far distance.

Originally an ancient Scottish game, golf spread all round the world in the nineteenth century when it became strictly an upper- and middle-class game, the workers serving as caddies, groundsmen, barmen and 'professionals'. Popularised by Lord Balfour in the twentieth century it became an important source of contact for small businessmen. With someone to carry the clubs it suited overweight middle-aged men and was respectable for women and the lower middle classes. The game became easier to play in 1902 when the solid gutta-percha ball was replaced by the rubber-cored and wound 'Haskell' ball, a mass-produced American invention.

'Golf with Kate and Bell.' Maggie Shaw is in the foreground. Kate and Bell Maclaren, daughters of a Kendal doctor, wear long dark skirts, white blouses and golfing hats. Behind the wall are Serpentine Woods, planted in 1790.

The club-house steps, 1907. The lower greens of Kendal golf course are in an old quarry, and a flight of steps gives access to the club-house above.

Tea on the golf links, 1906. The corrugated-iron shed with cardboard boxes stacked behind a window protected by chicken wire has now been replaced by a club-house. The flight of wooden steps has been replaced by an iron staircase, and the waitress whose tray is just visible on the left of the picture no longer serves afternoon tea.

Windermere, undated. The Japanese paper sunshade suggests a date of about 1910.

Windermere, south of the Nab. The steamboat in the bay is similar to Harold Walker's *Muriel*, known from a photograph of 1905. There were a few yachts converted to houseboats on Windermere at the turn of the century.

Malcolm Shaw and Harry Lyon shelling peas in the houseboat.

Boating party. Dark skirt, white blouse and straw hat or golf hat were appropriate on this outing.

Bowness Bay, Coronation Day, 1902. The coronation of Edward VII and Queen Alexandra, planned for 26 June 1902, was postponed only two days before the event because the King had appendicitis, then known as perityphlitis. The King underwent surgery on 17 June, when it was announced from Buckingham Palace that a large abscess had been successfully removed.

A week later, the Earl Marshall's office announced the indefinite postponement of the Coronation and the following day Kendal Town Council met to discuss the matter. It decided to take down all the decorations except those at Abbot Hall; to cancel the bands, the historical procession and the mayoral service at the parish church; to take down the bonfire and store the materials for future use; to proceed with the children's and old folks' treat at Abbot Hall; and to send an expression of sympathy to the King and Royal family.

Similar decisions were taken elsewhere and the day's events were muted. The Shaws went boating on Windermere.

Bowness Bay, 1902. The following is extracted from the *Westmorland Gazette*, 22 February 1902:

'There was another night's hard frost on Friday, the thermometer at eight o'clock on Saturday morning indicating 12 degrees of frost. Saturday was a busy day on the ice; large numbers of people came to Windermere by the ordinary trains and about 500 on an excursion from Lancaster and Morecambe. On Saturday there would be quite 7,000 people on the ice. By Sunday the ice opposite Bowness was nearly four inches thick and it was possible to skate from the Ferry to Lakeside. North of Millerground there was scarce a vestige of ice.

'In the forenoon the largest number of persons in Bowness Bay at one time would be scarcely more than 100 but in the afternoon the throng was greatly augmented. Heavily laden excursions came to Lake Side from the Furness district and many of these excursionists skated up to Bowness. On Sunday afternoon Mr Salkeld, booking clerk of Kendal, and a daughter of Mr Nathan Shepherd, skating on the line of the steamer track between Belle Isle and Henholme, went through the ice together. A "chain" was formed along the ice by Mr Nicholson and several other men and the two were quickly extricated. Both had gone overhead and the young woman was in a half-fainting condition. On Sunday a young man had his nose injured by falling against a companion's skate. He was taken into a boathouse bleeding profusely, a doctor was sent for and the injured nose was bound up.

'Several parties from Storrs disported themselves on the lake opposite there and found the ice as smooth as glass. People travelling between the Sawrey side and Bowness, either on foot or bicycle, have freely made use of the ice as a highway. It was curious to see barrowfuls of provisions being wheeled across the ice to the residence on Belle Isle.

'On Sunday and Monday night the frost was again keen and the danger flags were shifted further out from the Bay. During the afternoon the number of persons on the ice at one time might be between 2,000 and 3,000, the crowd being thickest off Fallbarrow Point on which Mr Raine had planted his refreshment marquee. The boat proprietors had turned their cushion-houses into cloak rooms, and the seats on the promenade had been lifted onto the ice. The Bijou Band were playing near Fallbarrow Point and it was estimated that the number present on the ice was between 8,000 and 10,000.'

The English Lake District has long attracted both professional and amateur photographers, the celebrated G.P. Abraham advertising his Keswick studio in the local newspaper as early as the 1860s. Professional photographers appear first in the Kendal directory of 1873 where Kelly lists William Moscrop, primarily a portrait photographer, and James Henry Hogg, an international prize winner for portrait and landscape work and a pioneer of photography since 1858. In the directories of 1885, 1894 and 1905 five professional photographers with studios in Kendal are listed and from the early 1900s Joseph Sawyers and James Ewan also emerge as photographers of street scenes, sold in their shops as postcards.

Margaret Shaw, hitherto unknown as a photographer, was a contemporary of these pioneers and at her wedding received a watercolour from Mrs James Hogg. She would have been familiar with photography of the highest standards.

This photograph shows Mr Brunskill in the garden at Underwood, Queen's Road, Kendal. His camera has a Thornton-Pickard roller shutter, a development of the 1890s. Margaret Shaw's diaries mention an evening spent with her friend Mary Littlewood at Brigsteer developing plates and tea parties at Laburnum Bank where Mr Sharpe took photographs. In 1912 she went with Malcolm Shaw, his close friend Harry Lyon, May Lyon and Jenny Quinn to a lecture at Kendal Museum on 'Colour Photography'. Photography was by then a popular middle-class pastime in Kendal, having been popularised, particularly amongst women, by Queen Alexandra's enthusiasm for the hobby.

7
OUTINGS

Split level, 1908. This building near Hawkshead church is still a popular photographic subject. Similar outside staircases were common in Kendal before the clearances of the 1960s.

Grizedale's refreshment rooms, 1908. Middlefell Place was the pioneer mountaineering centre for the Fell and Rock Climbing Club, founded in 1907. Gimmer Crag, Pavey Ark and Bowfell Buttress were all explored from here.

The Post Office, Patterdale, 1904. The little girls with the postcard stands have some jars of jam and a basket of eggs on their trestle table. The building, opposite the Glenridding Hotel, is now a private house.

The Bowder Stone, 1902. This immense boulder near the entrance to Borrowdale, the largest glacial erratic in the district, was believed by eighteenth- and nineteenth-century tourists to have rolled from the adjacent heights. Guide books give its vital statistics: length 60 feet, height 36 feet, circumference 84 feet, computed weight nearly 1800 tons.

In a letter written in 1807, Southey satirized its vulgarisation by a Mr Pocklington who nearby had 'built a little mock hermitage, set up a new druidical stone, erected an ugly house for an old woman to live in who is to show the rock, for fear travellers should pass underneath it without seeing it, cleared away all the fragments round it, and as it rests upon a narrow base, like a ship upon its keel, dug a hole underneath through which the curious may gratify themselves by shaking hands with the old woman.'

The photograph shows the heavy clothing customarily worn even for walking excursions, the men in jackets and waistcoats, high collars and ties; the women in shoe length skirts. None of the party is without a hat. The view from the summit of the Bowder Stone is mainly more rock and, today, the National Trust car park.

Watendlath, 1902. The cluster of hay barns in the photograph, the managed 'inbye' on the lowest slopes, and the gullied fells in the background reveal this hamlet as a pastoral settlement. There are abundant signs of rapid erosion on the rough grazing, following destruction of the forest cover. Wordsworth (1835) recalls the old people of nearby Wythburn saying that a squirrel might have gone from their chapel to Keswick without alighting on the ground. Here, that native tree-cover has gone, probably at the hands of charcoal burners; overgrazing has stopped it regenerating and soil erosion is active. To the left of the main gully in the centre of the picture the soil is breaking up into blocks as it slides downhill; on the right it has gone from the lower slopes and is still actively eroding above. On the right a plantation has stabilised most of the gully head but there are many breaks in the vegetation on the lower slopes. In the foreground bracken has invaded the inbye and rushes are spreading on the wetter ground. Wordsworth records that sycamore 'has long been the favourite of the cottagers; and with the fir, has been chosen to screen their dwellings'. Among the buildings here several fine sycamores and a 'fir' or Scots pine can be seen, and several of the larches which Wordsworth so detested.

Helvellyn, 1902. Edward Easton, whose name appears on the sign of the Nag's Head, and his wife Jane, were succeeded as licensees by the grandparents of Mr George Fisher of Keswick, who was born there in 1924. The inn was extremely popular both with locals and visitors arriving by horse charabanc from Ambleside. By 1929 the number of visitors attracted there was thought to have become a pollution risk to Thirlmere and the inn was converted to two cottages. These were eventually demolished but the kitchen gardens survive across the road next to Wythburn church.

The driver of the charabanc in low-crowned top hat stands in the road while the passengers mount and the ostler inspects the horses. A 'slipper' can be seen slung on chains below the departing vehicle. At the top of steep hills this iron shoe was placed in front of a rear wheel which was then driven on to it. The charabanc then skidded down the hill to safety. At Kirkstone Pass a boy was stationed at the top and another at the bottom of the hill to attach and remove the shoe. The boy at the top got a penny from the coachman and frequently a shower of pennies from apprehensive passengers. The boy at the bottom got a halfpenny and often burned his fingers on the hot shoe. The mounting ladder and a bucket for watering the horses can be seen beside the wall. Much of the charm of the inn comes from its twenty-paned sash windows and the oil-lit lantern.

Malcolm and Margaret Shaw and the Stevenettes refresh themselves at the rear of the pub with slices of lemon and Bell's Aerated Mineral Water, as advertised on the poster on the pub door. The stoneware bottle, labelled T. Bell, Ambleside, contained ginger beer. The lemonade is in Codd bottles, each with a glass marble in the neck, as patented by Mr Hiram Codd in 1870. Codd gave the English language a new word: 'codswallop' was a disparaging term used by beer and spirit drinkers for fizzy soft drinks.

The rock formation and the quarry waste indicate a path beside the Tilberthwaite green slate quarries, about 4 miles from Coniston railway station. Margaret Shaw's diary records a Guild outing to Coniston in June 1909.

The ride on the 'Ratty', 1908. The Ravenglass and Eskdale Railway, built to carry iron ore from Eskdale to Ravenglass, ended its life as an ore line when the Gill Force mines at the head of the dale closed in 1884. After a series of financial crises and take-overs, its life as a freight line was extended briefly in 1905, carrying granite from a quarry just below Boot at Beckfoot. In 1876 it had been licensed to carry passengers and a ride up Eskdale to Irton Green became a popular Bank Holiday weekend attraction. The line's two coaches were then supplemented by ore-tippers and freight wagons to accommodate mainly standing passengers. The side door wagon in the picture above is furnished with garden seats.

The picture below shows the 3 foot gauge track, the rear of one of the coaches and, on the left of the platform, the 'Waiting Hut', a wooden shelter with a sloping roof. The inspector who licensed the line for passenger use complained of the lack of toilet facilities at the halts. These were promised by the directors but 'forgotten' when the passenger service opened.

Boot Mill, 1908. From early medieval times, mills were owned by the lords of the manors and tenants were obliged to have their corn ground in their own lord's mill and pay 'mulcture' of between a twelfth and a twentieth part. A corn mill is believed to have operated at Boot since the thirteenth century and it was still a manorial mill in the seventeenth century. It was extended in the eighteenth century to include a second water wheel and when these photographs were taken it was still in use as a corn mill. It ground mainly oats, the staple diet of the population eaten as porridge and oatcakes, and a little barley for use as barley bread.

The mill and the miller's cottage were bought by Cumberland County Council in 1972 and opened to the public as a museum in 1976. To the right of the mill in the photographs is a packhorse bridge over which would have been brought peat from the fell above for heating the corn drying kiln, haematite from the ore mines, and locally woven woollen cloth.

Sandside, 1907. These hardy picnickers perched on uncomfortable rocks have produced cups of tea all round. The paraphernalia includes matches (right of the bucket) and newspaper (extreme right) for starting the fire, and milk in a medicine bottle.

Silloth, 1902. The pierrots. The concert party in the shelter of the dunes has a piano and some kitchen chairs as stage properties and pierrot costumes, three of them with tall pierrot hats, and has drawn a crowd of over a hundred. To the left of the picture are the bath houses where visitors could take hot and cold salt water baths. The plate has been double exposed.

Donkey rides at Silloth, with Stephen Shaw and the Middleton twins.

Silloth, 1902. The view to Scotland. Mrs Shaw in her rustic chair would have had a superb view across the Firth – pink seathrift flowering on the saltmarshes with the hazy hills of Dumfries and Kirkcudbright on the skyline.

Silloth itself would have added interest. There were few houses there until 1857, but with the coming of the railway they had sprung up in all directions. From the wooden pier steamers sailed out past the wooden lighthouse to Dublin or Liverpool and, seen in the background, the two hotels provided billiard rooms and livery stables, both close to the golf links and the bandstand.

8

OUT & ABOUT IN KENDAL

One of the most remarkable personalities amongst the Shaws' friends was Charles Fildes, pioneer of steam boats on Lake Windermere, seen here in the back lane between 'Overdale' and Windermere Road. His family appears in the Manchester street directories of 1855 and 1861 as tin, copper and zinc packing case manufacturers and authorised gas fitters. Charles, also a tin plate manufacturer, is known to local historians as the builder in 1850 of the *Fairy Queen*, the first private paddle steamer recorded on Windermere. He lived at Gill Bank, north of Colt House near Hawkshead (p. 67) with his wife and nine children of whom, in 1891, the eldest was twenty-two and the youngest a baby. Not surprisingly he then moved to Kendal to 'Overdale', a six bedroomed house on Kendal Green. According to his son, Arthur Fildes, he was a familiar sight riding his tricycle to the railway station for the train to Manchester.

The motorbike in the photographs, EC 152, is listed in the records of Westmorland vehicle registrations held in the Cumbria Record Office in Kendal as a Coventry Notette, registered in 1904 and owned by Charles Fildes. He was seventy in that year. Mrs Fildes, Charles Fildes' third wife, is frequently mentioned in Margaret Shaw's diaries, exchanging calls and visits to tea or supper. The two went together to a Wesleyan bazaar, a furniture sale at Dalton and on cycle rides to Underbarrow and Bowness and occasionally to church at St Thomas's. Mrs Fildes seems to have been a popular hostess, the diaries recording that in 1909 'She had all the women in her district to tea in the garden before the cycle parade in the evening' and that, in 1912, her New Year's Eve party went on until 2 a.m.

On 23 April 1900, a 1,000 mile car trial run by the Automobile Club started from Hyde Park Corner on a course which passed through Bristol, Birmingham, Manchester, Kendal, Carlisle, Edinburgh, Newcastle, Leeds, Sheffield, Nottingham and back to London, each town marking the end of a day's stage. Eighty vehicles set out but only sixty reached Manchester, some having succumbed to a hill climbing test in Derbyshire. From Preston to Kendal a county surveyor led the way in a pilot car and on Monday 5 May, in mid-afternoon, a 12 horse power car driven by the Hon. C.S. Rolls, a prominent participant in races in France, led the cavalcade along Mercers' Lane into the Market Hall, where it formed an exhibition for the public until the following day. According to the *Westmorland Gazette*, 'the cars were of all kinds, patterns, sizes, weights and colours – mostly driven by petrol though two or three had steam as the motive power. There were vehicles of the very latest make and of varied horse power by both continental and English makers from the not-unattractive tricycle to the cars of large and lumbering dimensions with a capacity of 12 horse power. The travellers were dust-begrimed and had anything but smartness in their appearance but what else could be expected with so many ponderous and swiftly travelling vehicles following closely in each other's wake and dust showers?' The exhibition raised between £15 and £20 for the War Fund. Every vehicle which completed the distance and showed an average speed of 5 miles an hour was awarded a prize of £10. In this photograph, the Hon. C.S. Rolls is saluting as his car approaches the Town Hall. With the car-designer Henry Royce, he founded Rolls-Royce Ltd six years later. In 1910 he flew both ways across the English Channel without stopping, and in the same year he became the first English victim of aviation when he was killed in a flying accident at Bournemouth.

The Bioscope, New Road, *c*. 1901. This early form of cinema reached the working-class public in Kendal via a fairground booth on the New Road. The cinema pioneer showman Randal Williams caused a sensation with his bioscope show at Hull in 1896 and by the early years of the century his shows appeared regularly at Dalton Whitsuntide fair. The title beside the booth reads 'Savage South Africa. The war in the Transvaal as seen in the American Bioscope.' This spectacular film with 'savages and horses specially trained' was shown at the Greater Britain Exhibition at Earl's Court in 1899. At this date most films were of travel in exotic locations, and at 1*d* or 2*d* tickets were cheap.

Sanger's Circus, Finkle Street, 1901. In the Boxer rebellion of 1900, bands of Chinese nationalists, known as 'Boxers', besieged the foreign legations in Pekin and murdered European missionaries and thousands of Chinese Christian converts. The following year, 'Lord' John Sanger and Sons' travelling circus exhibited in a marquee 'REAL CHINESE BOXERS that actually took part in the Siege of the British Legation in Pekin, dressed in full National Costume'. Seen here in procession up Kendal's Finkle Street, the circus also staged 'The Great Football Match – Elephant v Man', in which William Sill, a forward in the Kendal Hornets, competed against the elephant for a 'massive goblet'.

Kendal railway station, 1907. Stephen Shaw is seated. Litter on the tracks seems to have been a problem then as it is now.

'When the Boys came home'. At 4.20 a.m. on 30 April 1901, the 1st Active Service Volunteer Company of the Border Regiment arrived in Carlisle from Southampton on its return from service in the Boer War. After a welcome on the station platform by the Mayor and Corporation and a tumultuous reception in the streets by the citizens, the Company reached the Drill Hall for breakfast. A formal welcome from the Town Hall steps followed, with speeches from the Mayor and their officer Captain Thompson. Led by a military band, the company marched through the packed streets to the Cathedral for a Thanksgiving Service and thence to the Castle. There, after further speeches, the men were each presented with a card picture of Table Bay from the Mayor of Cape Town, who had been unable to present them personally in South Africa because of an outbreak of bubonic plague.

Returning to the station, the men from Kendal, Milnthorpe, Staveley, Windermere and the Lake District, thirty-seven in all, boarded a train for Kendal, due to arrive there at 12.20. At Kendal station, the Town Band, unaware that the Volunteers' train was late, greeted the surprised passengers of the ordinary 12.28 with the rousing strains of 'The Conquering Heroes'. When the men finally arrived, the band's repeat performance was entirely drowned by the cheers of the reception party and the massed crowds.

Led by a colonel, the Company marched down Wildman Street, New Road and Aynam Road to the Drill Hall for a substantial dinner, and thence back via Kent Street and Finkle Street to the front of the Town Hall. Here they were addressed from the balcony by the Mayor and Mr J. Somervell, before proceeding with a bodyguard of Active Service Volunteers in double file down Highgate to the parish church for another Thanksgiving Service. After a longish service and sermon and tributes to those who had died of fever and in action, they returned to the Drill Hall and dismissed.

Reassembled in St George's Hall in the evening at a soirée to which the volunteers' wives were admitted at a reduced charge, they were addressed twice more, by a major and by Mr W.D. Crewdson, congratulated again on their patriotism, and each was presented by Mrs Wakefield with a silver gilt watch. Dancing then began and continued until the early hours of the following morning.

9

POSTSCRIPT

In 1916, at the age of forty-one, Margaret Shaw married John Bewley of Causa Grange, a near neighbour of her mother's family. The wedding was at St Jude's church, Raughton Head, close to her Aunt Ettie's home at Sebergham. Margaret had become a popular member of her social circle, and the *Kendal Mercury and Times*, reporting the event, recorded down to the last tea cosy and crochet doily the eighty presents received from her many friends. After a honeymoon tour of Chester, Leamington, Kenilworth, Stratford, Banbury and Oxford, including an unsuccessful attempt to visit Blenheim Palace, the couple returned to Causa Grange. John Bewley continued to farm the family estate, mainly as mixed stock and arable farming but with cash crops from three orchards and 3 acres of strawberries. Breeding sheep were bought in Scotland and brought by rail to Curthwaite station, and cattle and sheep from Causa Grange were sold mainly at Hope's Auction Mart in Wigton. Produce from the garden and orchards was sent to Manchester by train from Curthwaite.

Causa Grange was a substantial house with five reception rooms and five bedrooms, and with plenty of money and an upbringing amongst architects Margaret soon had it thoroughly modernised and refurbished in preparation for her social role as the wife of a gentleman farmer. Her summer picnics, lavishly supplied with salmon and refreshing delicacies, were only surpassed by her Christmas whist parties at which fires would be lit in all the rooms and goose with all imaginable adjuncts was served to upwards of thirty people.

Margaret kept up with her old friends in Kendal where, after her parents' day, she kept on her room at 157 Stricklandgate and another in the Bewley family's house in Carlisle. Every year she and her housekeeper made four Christmas cakes, one for her own household, one for her brother Malcolm's family and two for the annual Christmas bazaar run by her old Presbyterian friends at the church in Sandes Avenue.

During the war, getting to Kendal from Rosley was difficult but she would set off on foot and hitch-hike either to the railway or by road over Shap. On the fourth Friday of every month, the AA superintendent for the area came through Rosley and a dozen eggs changed hands as the price of a ride into Newcastle for a shopping expedition. Another notable lift from Rosley was to a wedding in Curthwaite, at which Margaret arrived in her best outfit on the back of a coal lorry.

Shopping was done mainly in Wigton and Carlisle where any surplus produce from Causa

Grange was sold in the markets. To get to Wigton, John Willie Pearson's bus was used. It had wooden wheels with rubber tyres and an iron ladder at the back up to a roof rack on to which baskets of butter and eggs, apples, plums, strawberries, gooseberries and daffodils were loaded. Passengers climbed up a step into the back of the bus and stepped over sacks, calves and baskets of chickens in the centre aisle to reach their seats. John Willie's service ended in 1941 to be succeeded by a Tuesday market-day-only bus run between Wigton and Penrith by Ernest Harkness. This was supplemented on Wednesdays and Saturdays by Cumberland Motor Services, which ran between Wigton and Carlisle. Reaching Rosley at 9.15 it continued via Curthwaite and Thursby to Carlisle, returning at 2 p.m.

In 1936, Margaret's transport problems were eased by the purchase of an 18 horse power Wolseley, driven by Johnson the chauffeur, who doubled as gardener/handyman. In it she promptly went to see the *Queen Mary* launched and, two years later, the laying of the keel of the *Queen Elizabeth* and the Glasgow Exhibition.

The couple had no children, but adopted a daughter who was sent off as a boarder to Keswick Grammar School before joining the Women's Auxiliary Air Force and marrying an RAF pilot. In 1939, at the very beginning of the Second World War, the Bewleys took in a family of five evacuee children from Newcastle – Eleanor, John, Ronnie, Alma and Iris Fenwick.

Margaret's two nephews remember her vividly as a non-stop organiser of exciting holiday expeditions. Saturday morning trips to Carlisle were undertaken with the boys squeezed in amongst the boxes and baskets of farm produce which filled the car and the drop-down iron rack behind. On shopping expeditions to Newcastle they were dropped off at the docks and left to their own devices, or sufficiently funded to explore the city's tramway system. On a railway expedition to Glasgow, one of the boys arrived with his aunt in Glasgow but his brother turned up in Edinburgh, having been in the lavatory in the wrong section of the train when it divided at Carstairs.

These outings were not all equally entertaining. After a Sunday afternoon lunch party at Causa Grange, Margaret took the boys to hear 'Messiah' in Carlisle cathedral. Missing the bus at Thursby, they walked the whole 10 miles in the pouring rain, the boys spending the evening in the Presbytery trying to get dry while Margaret sat dripping through the performance. The evening concluded, they set off by bus to Thursby and a final 5 mile walk home, still in the drenching rain.

Margaret's passion for outings was not confined to home territory. The Hotel Britannique in the Avenue Victoria was a favourite *pied-à-terre* in Paris from before the First World War and she returned there for her brother's silver wedding in 1947. In the 1920s they saw the Passion Play in Oberammergau, and bought a basket there which subsequently hung from a beam in the housemaid's room at Causa Grange. When it caught fire when an oil lamp Margaret was lighting got out of hand, she described it on her insurance claim as 'bought from Jesus'.

All Margaret's expeditions had a point to them – in Lucerne to buy a particular sort of pottery she collected decorated with blue cornflowers; to see the St Bernard dogs at the hospice in the St Bernard pass; to hear monks chant Vespers in a monastery. During the food rationing days after the Second World War she made a point of travelling home via Lille where she bought the butter and other ingredients needed for the next batch of Christmas cakes.

Margaret never learned to drive and after the death of her husband in 1945 her nephews were expected to drive the car on these expeditions. They remember her invariably dressed in stout tartan outfits of skirt, jacket and tam-o-shanter of which she had versions in red, green and blue. The post-war currency allowance for foreign travel being only £25 she conserved this for shopping by taking most of her food with her and sleeping in the car. On a visit to Annecy she settled down for the night in the car park in the middle of the Grand Place, to wake up next morning surrounded by the locals erecting their market stalls. They obligingly pushed her car on to the pavement where her nephew and his wife, returning from their hotel, found her beside it happily brewing tea on a primus stove. Adventurous and independent to the last, Margaret Bewley died in 1963 at the age of eighty-eight, to be buried with her husband in Rosley churchyard.

When plate cameras became obsolete she turned to roll film and continued taking photographs up to the Second World War when film became difficult to buy. Only her glass plate negatives taken before her marriage have survived but these, the stuff of any family album, now provide insights into the middle-class life of a time when ample leisure, an adequate income and the new mobility of bicycles and trains enabled such families to enjoy the freedom of the *belle époque*.

FAMILY TREE

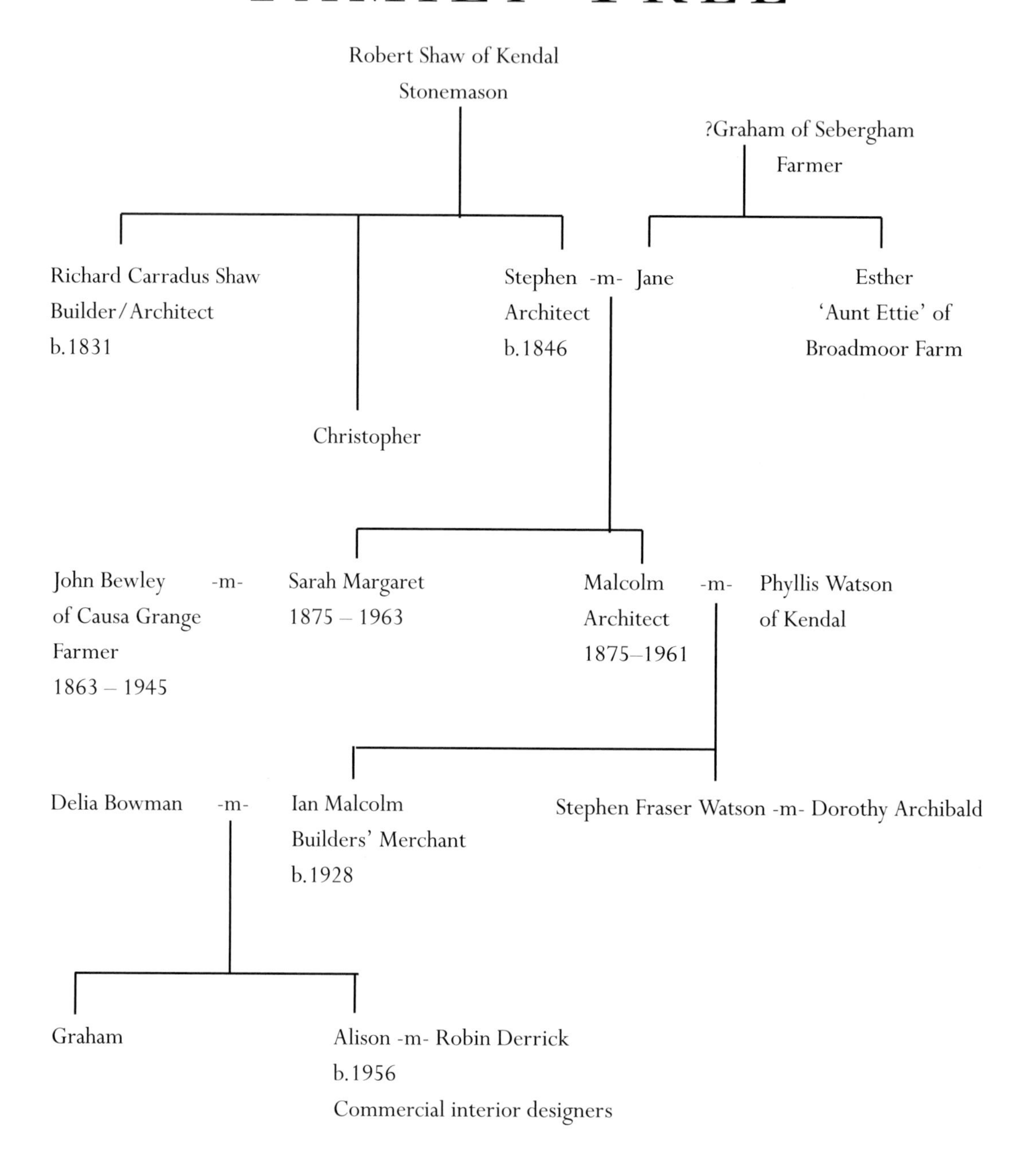

Robert Shaw of Kendal
Stonemason
?Graham of Sebergham
Farmer
Richard Carradus Shaw
Builder/Architect
b.1831
Christopher
Stephen -m- Jane
Architect
b.1846
Esther
'Aunt Ettie' of
Broadmoor Farm
John Bewley -m-
of Causa Grange
Farmer
1863 – 1945
Sarah Margaret
1875 – 1963
Malcolm -m- Phyllis Watson
Architect
1875–1961
of Kendal
Delia Bowman -m-
Ian Malcolm
Builders' Merchant
b.1928
Stephen Fraser Watson -m- Dorothy Archibald
Graham
Alison -m- Robin Derrick
b.1956
Commercial interior designers

SOURCES

Chapter 2: The Shaws of Kendal

Barker, P., Marsh, J., et al, *Victorian Architects of Kendal* (Abbot Hall Art Gallery, 1990). Unpublished information kindly supplied by Alison Shaw

Chapter 3: The Rosley Connection

Rosley Estate papers, Cumbria Record Office, Carlisle, *DX/131* (deposited by Major A.J. Dickinson)

Pearsall, R., *Edwardian Life and Leisure* (David and Charles, 1973)

Kelly's Directory of Cumberland and Westmorland (1894)

McIntire, W.T., 'Cumberland in the Past: Rosley and its Story', *Cumberland News* (June 1938)

Richards, J. and MacKenzie, J.M., *The Railway Station, A Social History* (OUP, 1986)

Staff, F., *The Penny Post, 1680–1918* (Lutterworth Press, 1964)

Thompson, F., *Lark Rise to Candleford* (OUP, 1945)

Winter, G., *The Golden Years, 1903–1913* (David and Charles, 1975)

Bishop, J., 'Social History of Edwardian Britain', *Illustrated London News* (A. Robertson, 1977)

Cole, G.D.H., *A Short History of the British Working Class Movement, 1789–1947* (Allen and Unwin, 1948)

Chapter 4: Domestic Life

Marfin, L., *Popular Leisure in the Lake Counties* (Manchester University Press, 1990)

Walton, J.K., 'Mad Dogs and Englishmen: the Conflict over Rabies in Late Victorian England', *Journal of Social History* (13 (2), 1979–80)

Geoffrey Thompson has provisionally identified the photograph on p. 53 as the Tivoli Tea Room, from a postcard of 1899 that shows the name of the tea room on the upper-floor oriel window, which now bears the name of the Liberal Club

Dutton, R., *The Victorian Home* (Bracken Books, 1954)

Cynthia Kelsall has kindly identified the garden plants

Chapter 5: Fashion

The horse-drawn vehicles have been kindly identified by the Bradford Industrial Museum and the Yorkshire Museum of Carriages and Horse Drawn Vehicles. Additional information is from Smith, D.J., *Discovering Horse-Drawn Carriages* (Shire Publications, 1985)

Sichel, M., *The Edwardians: Costume Reference 7* (Batsford, 1978)

Robinson, J., *The Golden Age of Style: Art Deco Fashion Illustration* (Orbis, 1976)

Raverat, G., *Period Piece: A Cambridge Childhood* (Faber, 1960)

Chapter 6: The Social Round

Beeton, Mrs, *All About Cookery* (Ward, Lock and Bowden, 1894)

Upper photograph on p. 109 kindly identified by Stephen Greenwood

Cycling information from The Mark Hall Cycle Museum, Harlow

Tennis information from The Wimbledon Lawn Tennis Museum

Westmorland Gazette, 28 June 1902

Lower photograph on p. 122: personal communication, G. Pattinson

Camera information on p. 128 from The National Museum of Photography

Chapter 7: Outings

Upper photograph on p. 130 kindly identified by Harry Griffin

Wordsworth, W., *A Guide Through the District of the Lakes in the North of England* (Hudson and Nicholson, 1835)

Davies, W.J.K., *The Ravenglass and Eskdale Railway* (David and Charles, 1981)

Information about the Nag's Head on p. 133 from G. Fisher

Chapter 8: Out & About in Kendal

Pattinson, G.H., *The Great Age of Steam on Windermere* (Windermere Nautical Trust Ltd, 1981)

Westmorland Gazette, 20 April 1901 and 4 May 1901